Adult Coloring Book

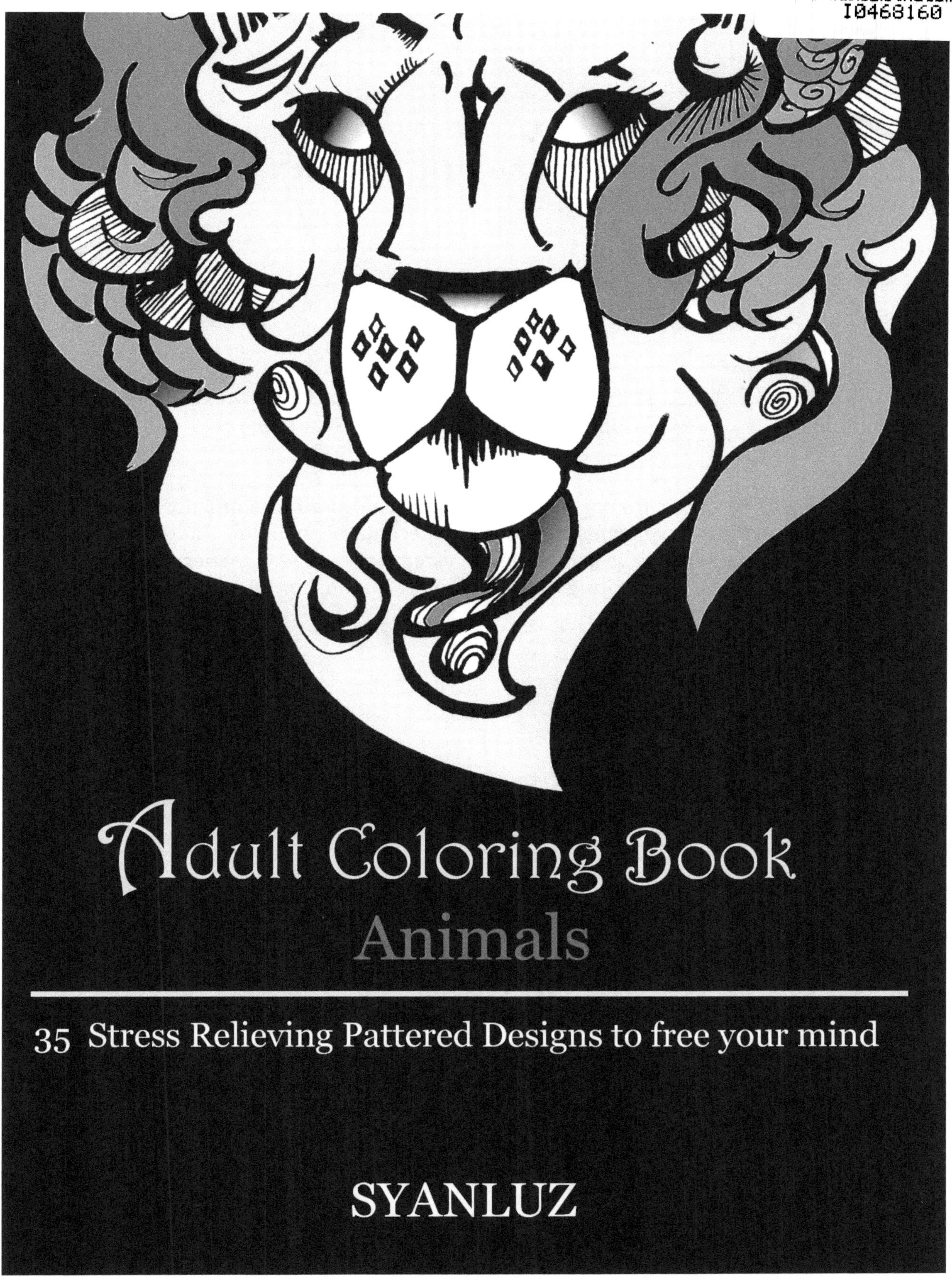

Animals

35 Stress Relieving Pattered Designs to free your mind

SYANLUZ

Adult coloring book

Animals

35 stress-relieving pattern designs to free your mind
©Copyright February 2016 by SyanLuz

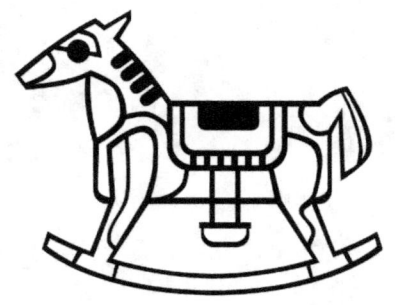

This book is perfect for you. As you are well aware, it is easier to put out a small fire then to extinguish a raging inferno. Similarly, small doses of stress are easier to control than large amount of stress that has built up over a period of time. One Medical Dr. stated " it is cruel that we make the daily practice of stress management a priority in our busy lives."

The aim of making a daily practice of stress management is twofold. First, it how to reduce the stressful triggers in life that can be reduced. And second, it helps control our response to the stresses that are unavoidable.

One practice that helps against stress management is coloring. Stress on the body can cause, Headaches, Tooth grinding, Neck pain, Heart disease, Ulcers, Back pain, Muscle spasms. DR .Joe Pearson, a brain scientist at the University of New South Wales in Australia spoke about the therapeutic effect of coloring stating: Concentrating on coloring and image may facilitate the replacement of negative thoughts and images with pleasant ones. That is exactly what we want to change, negative with positive ones. This will help you to that end.

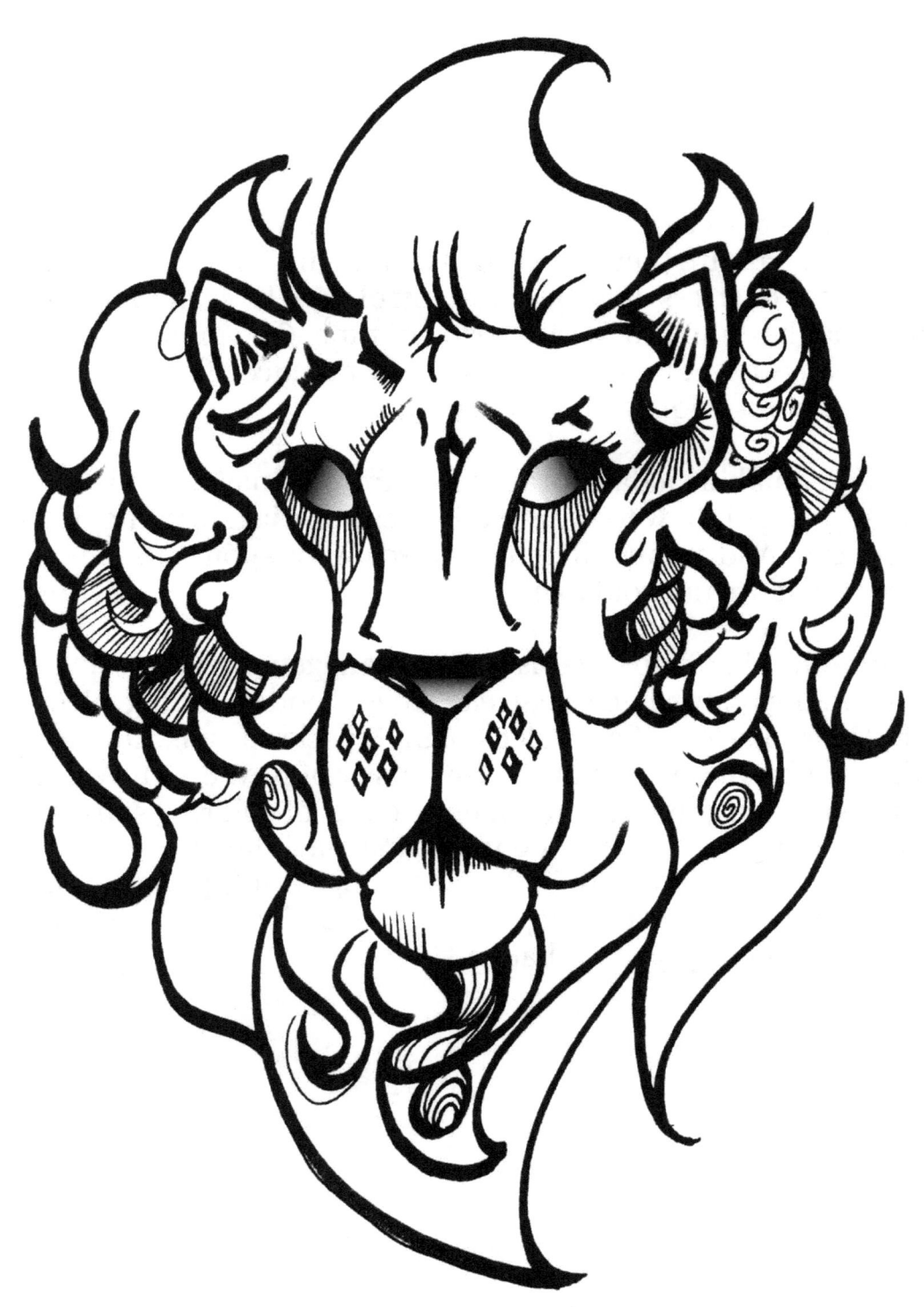

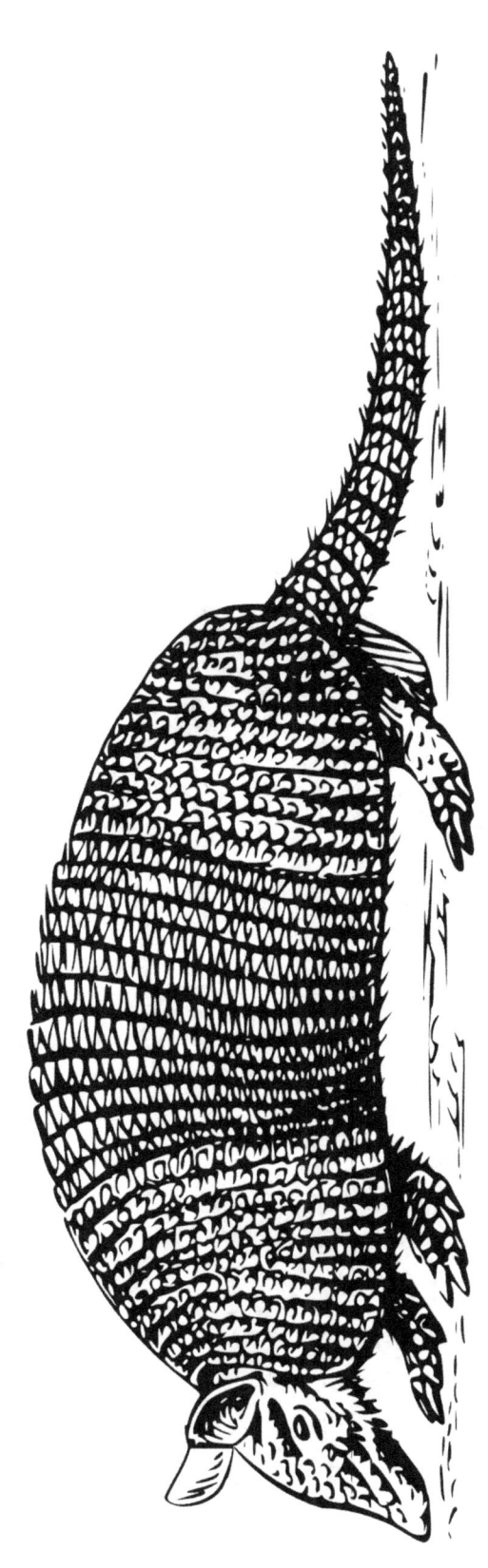

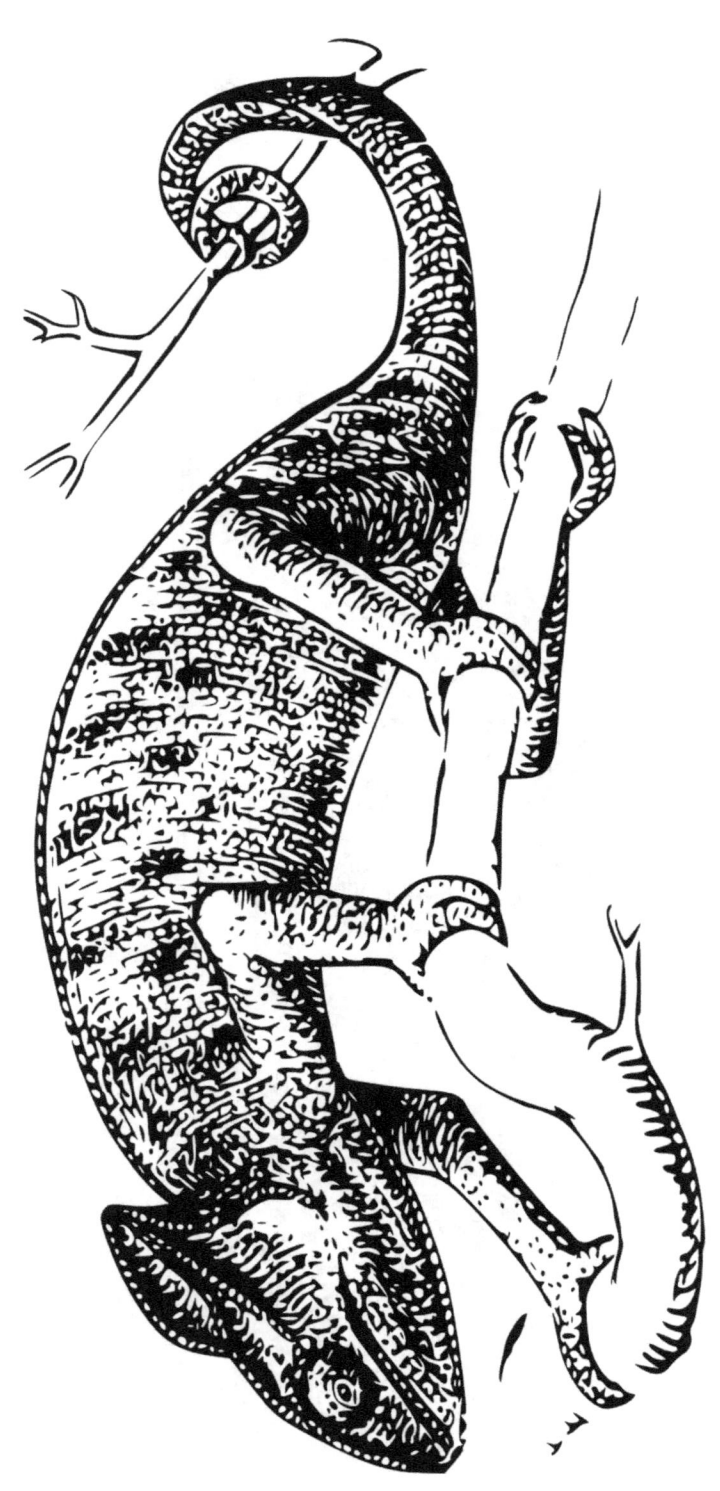

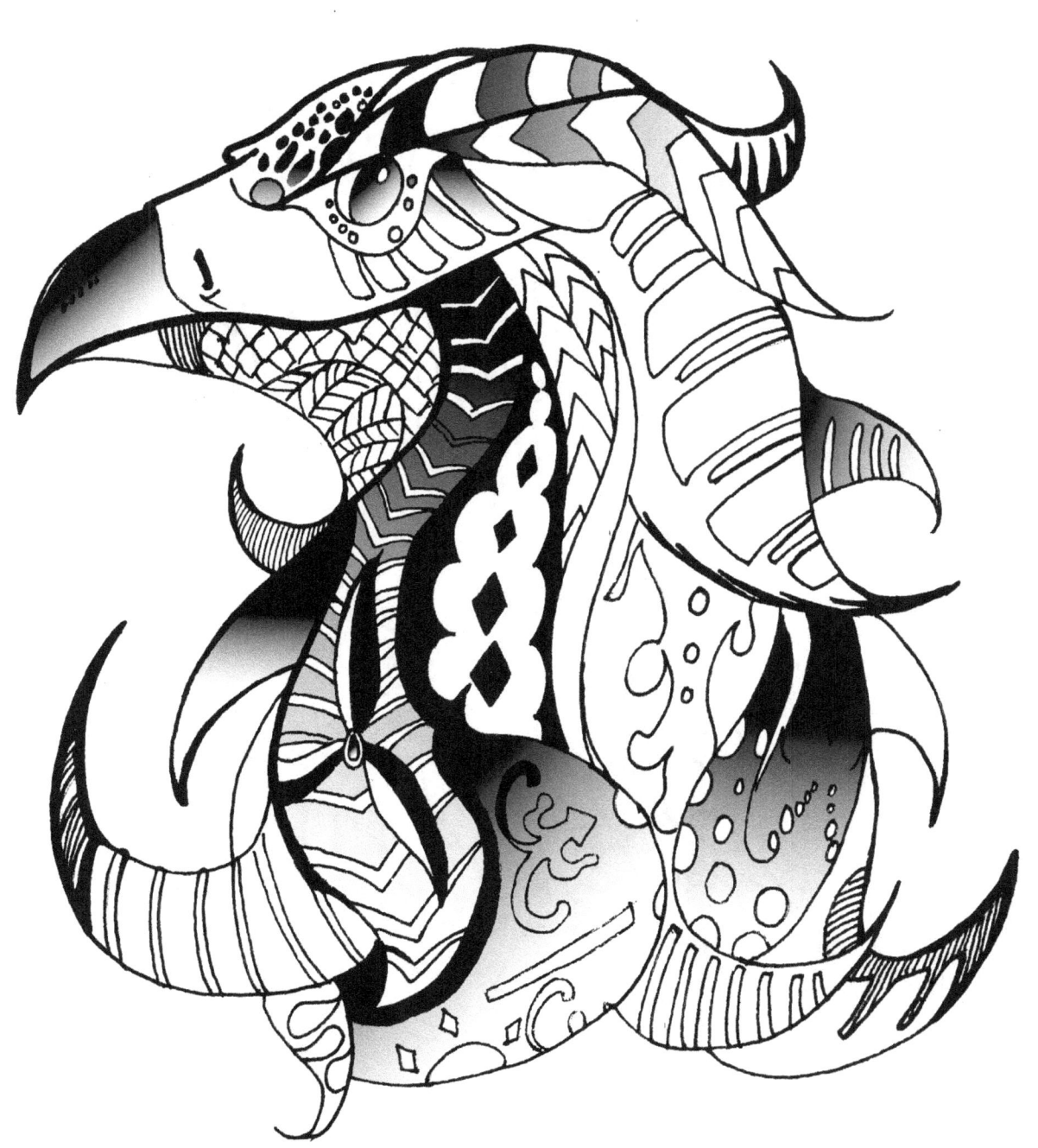

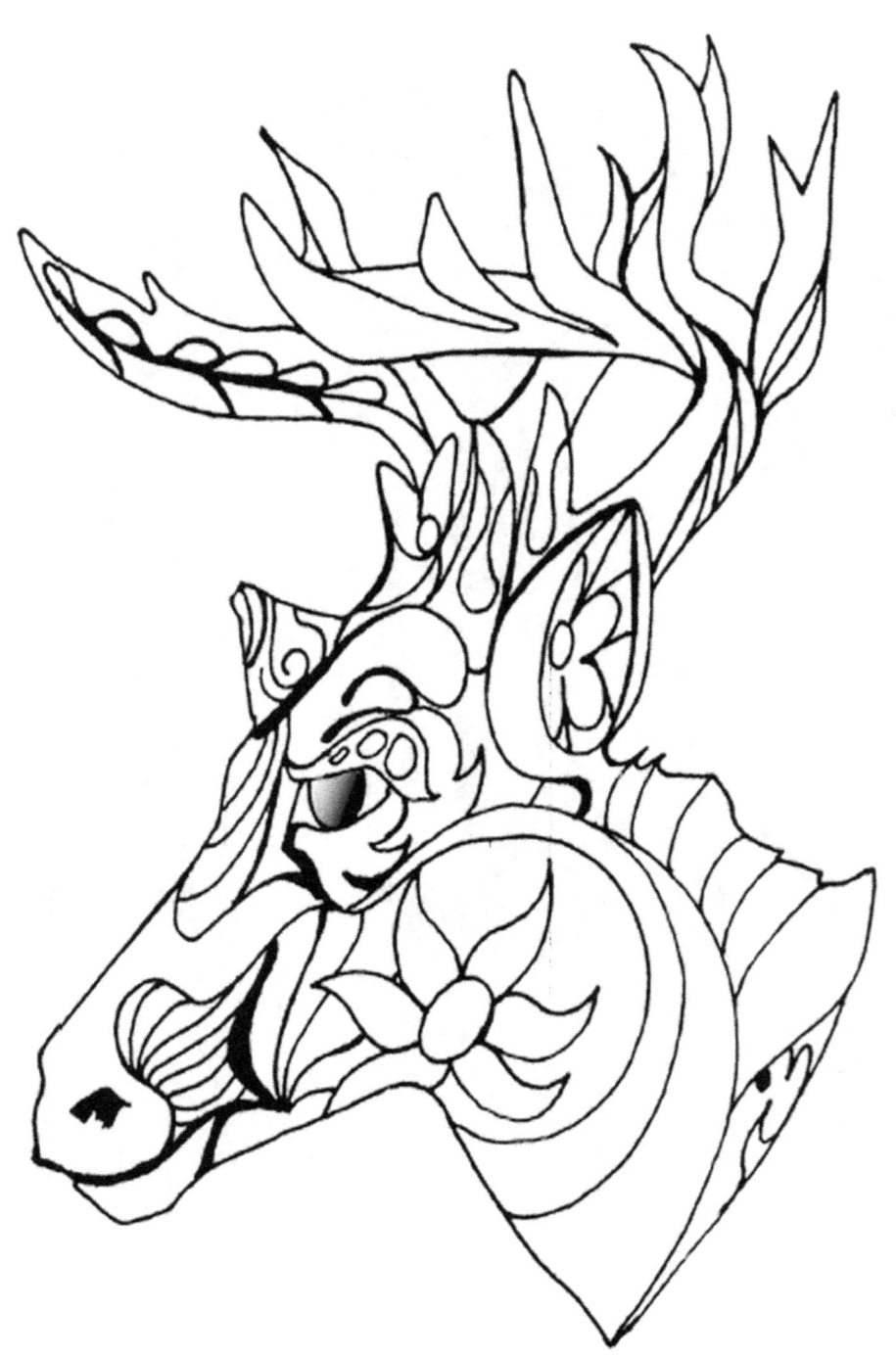

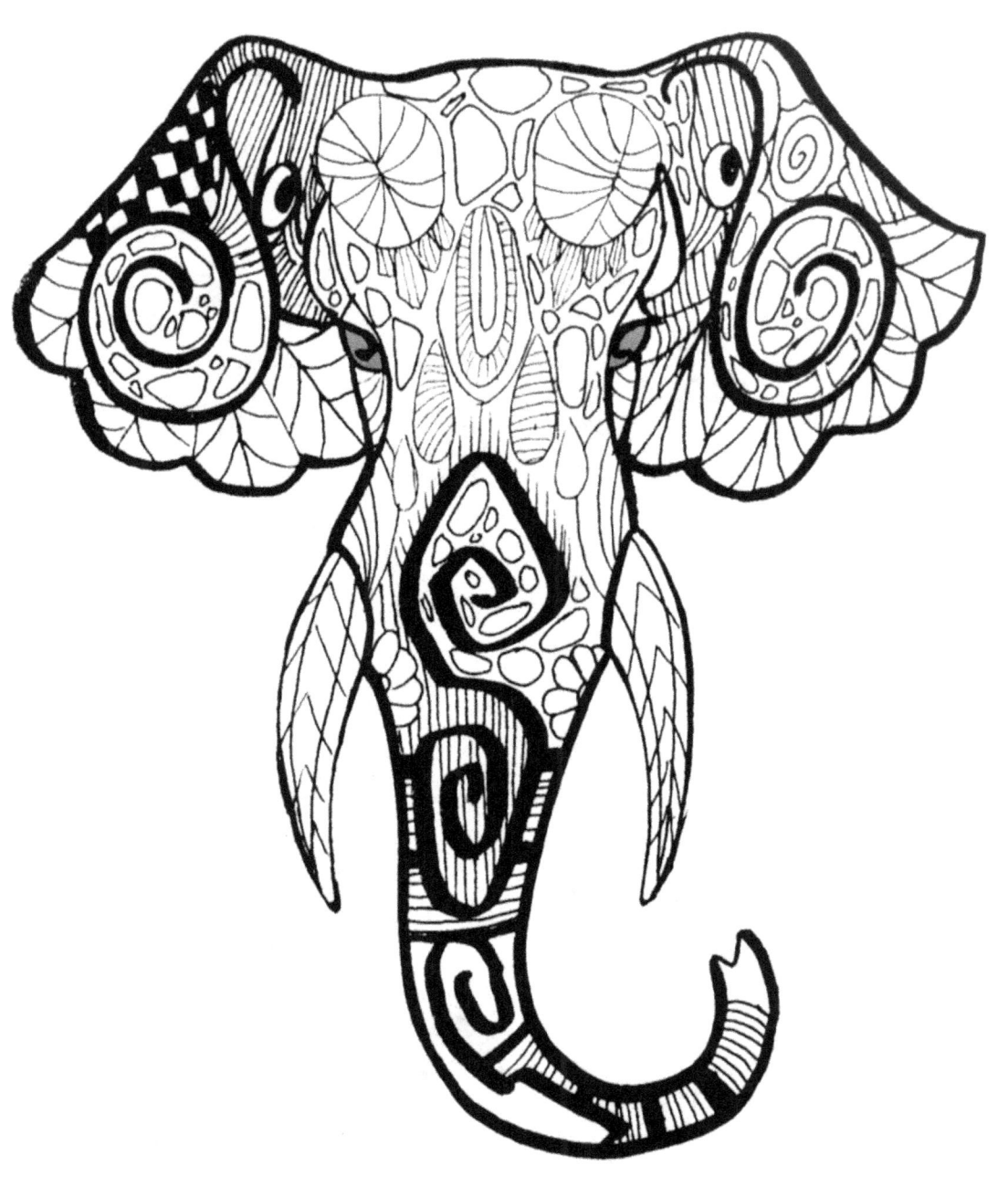

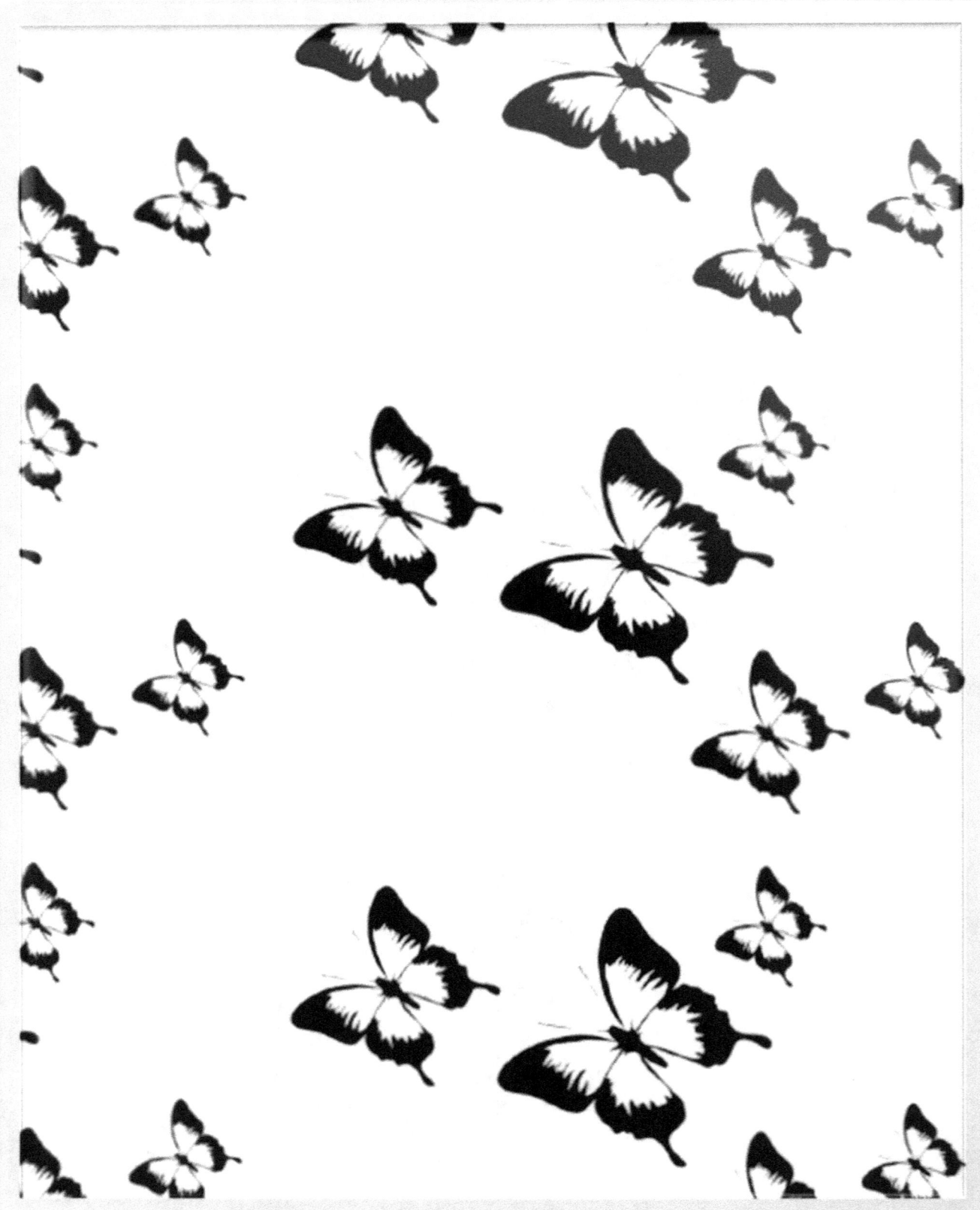

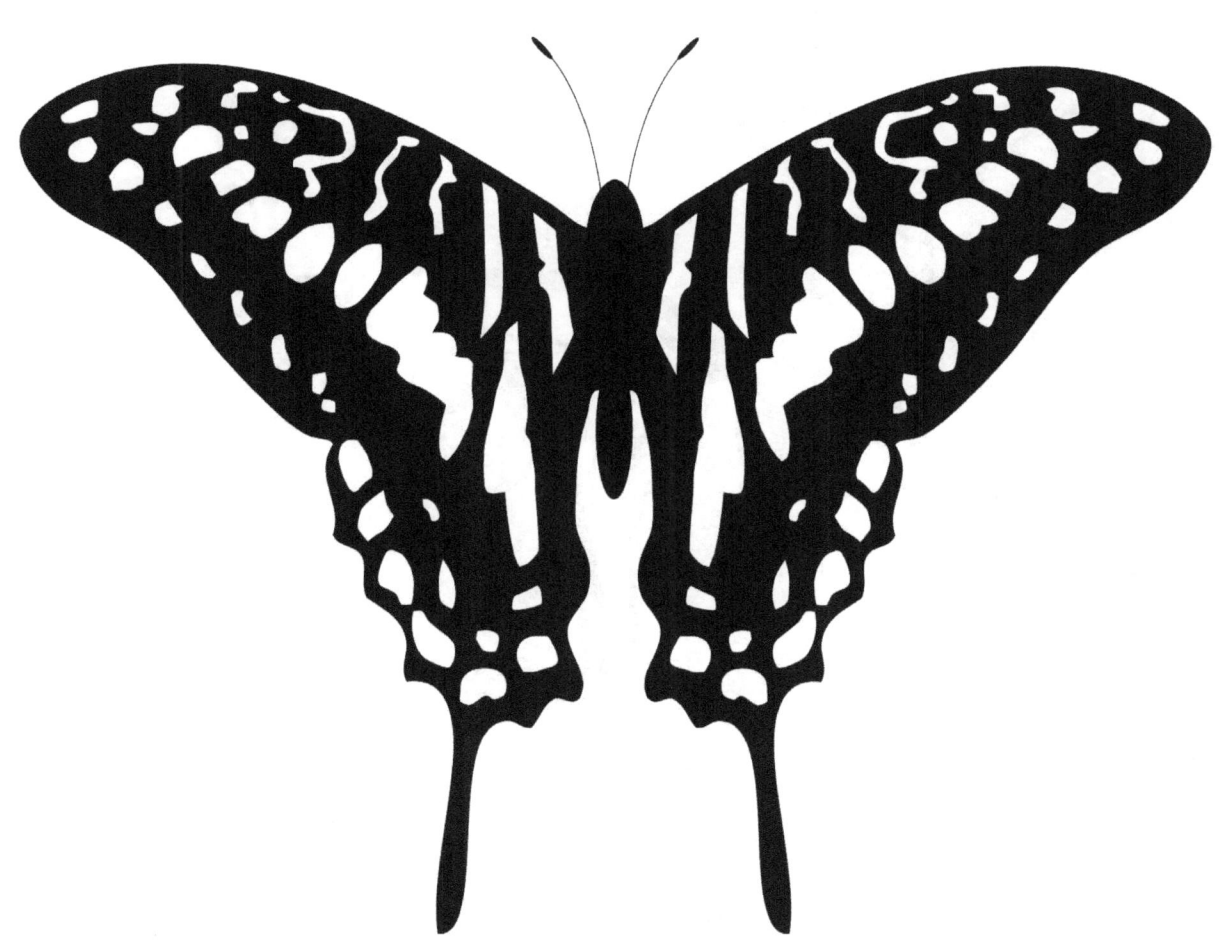

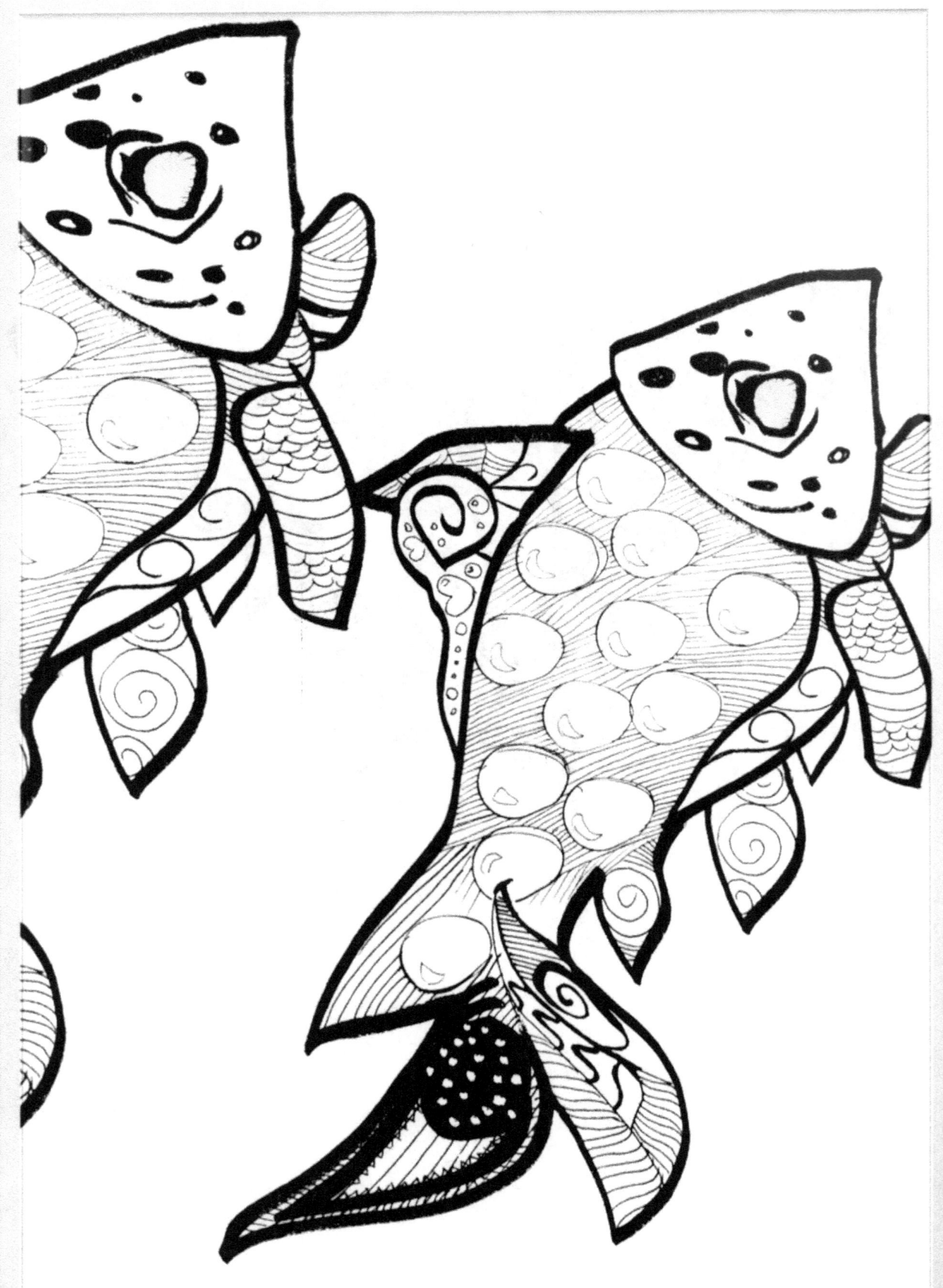

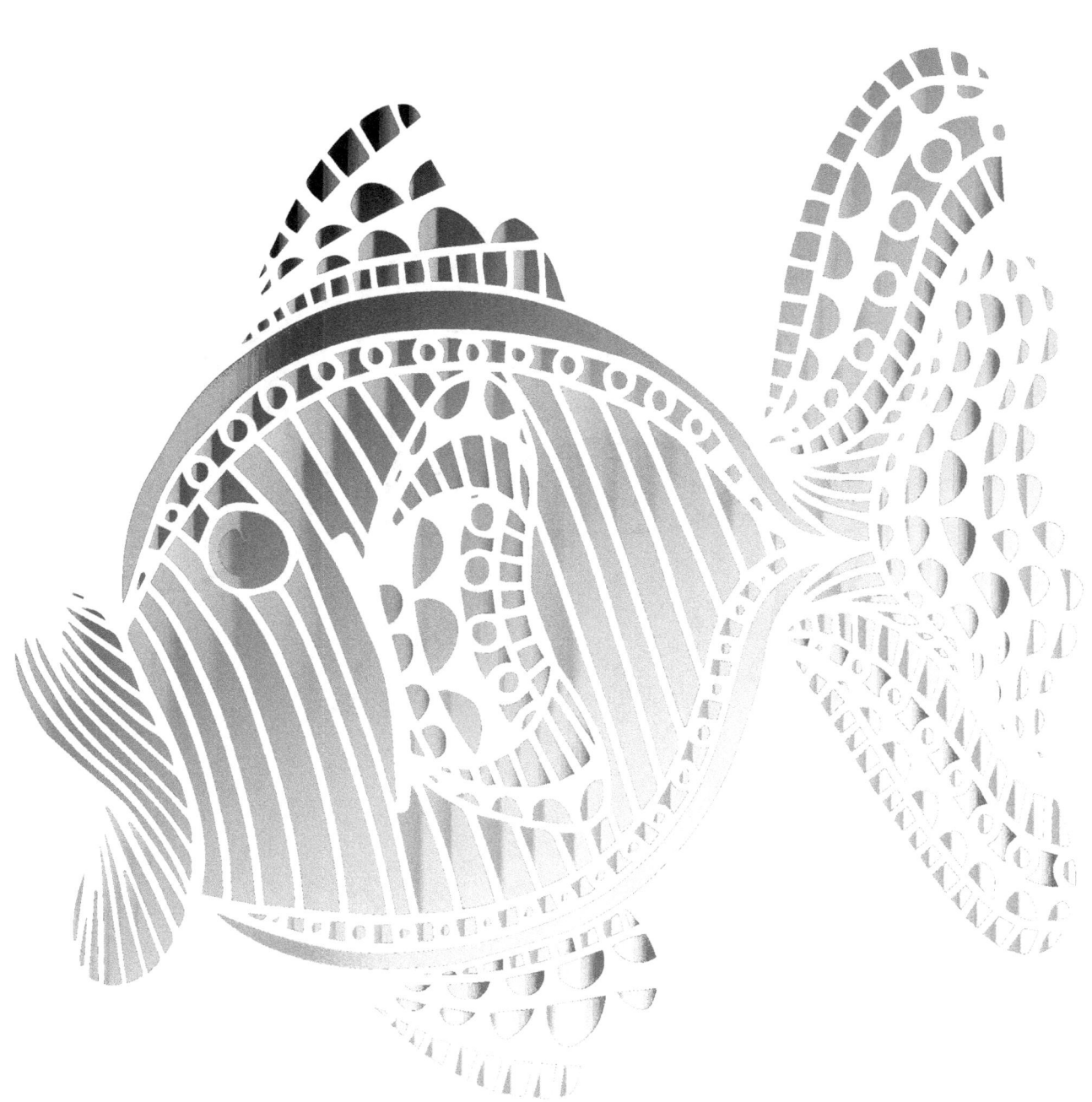

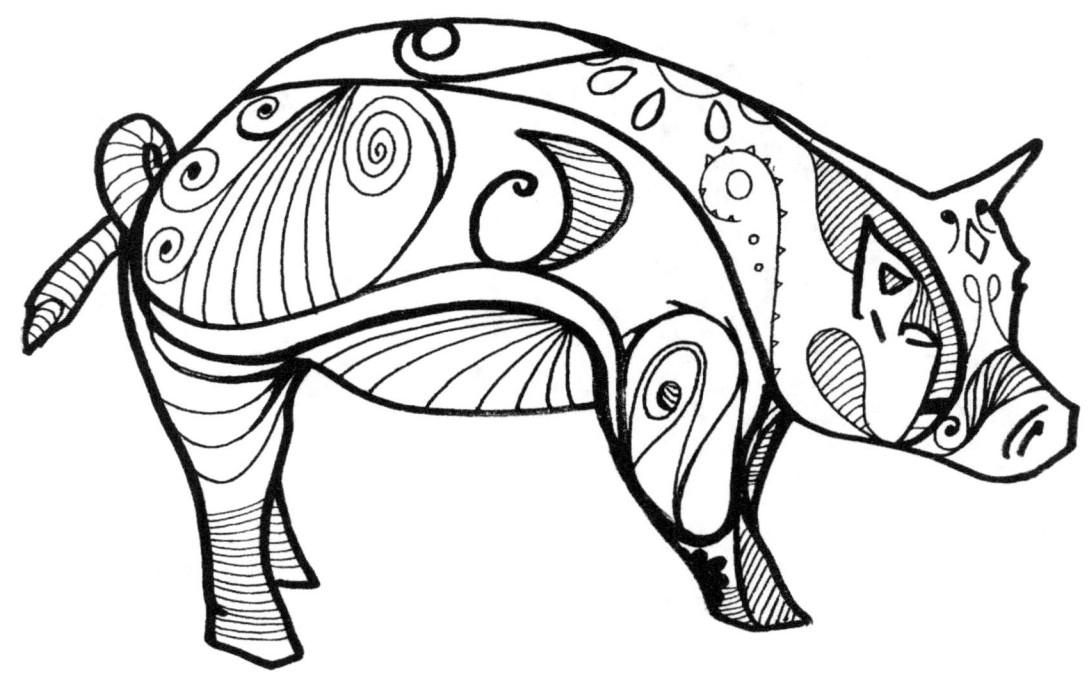

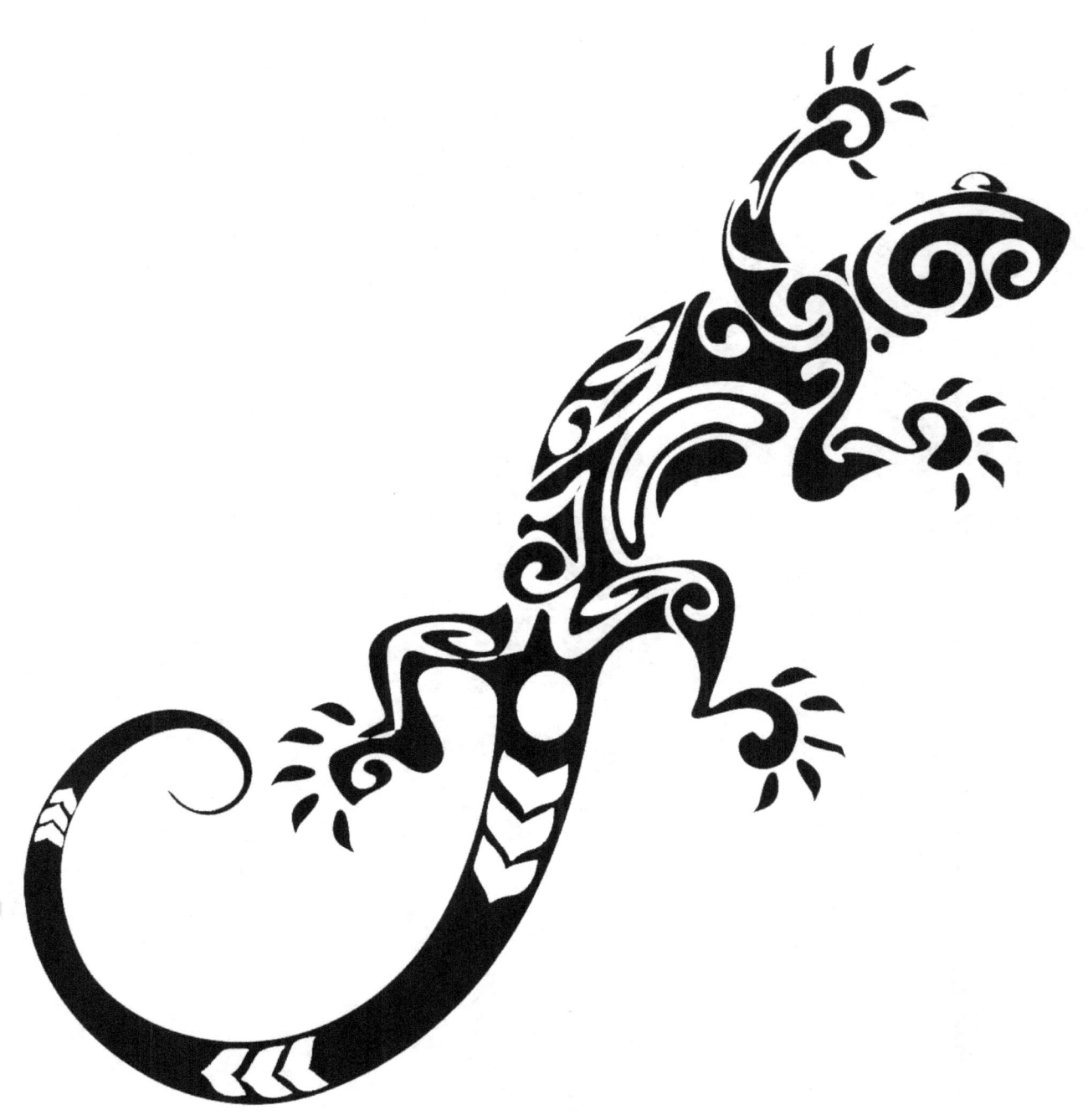

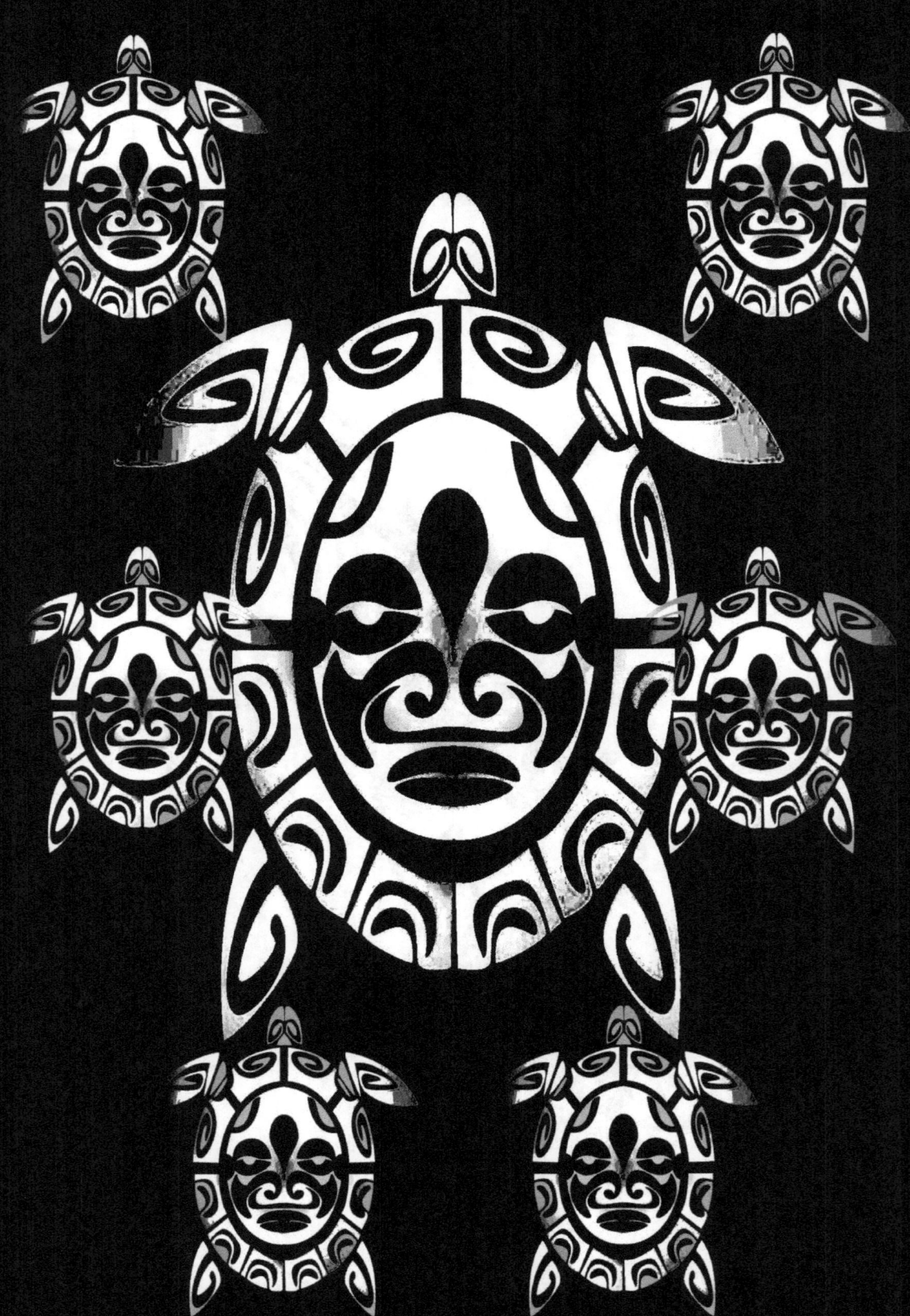

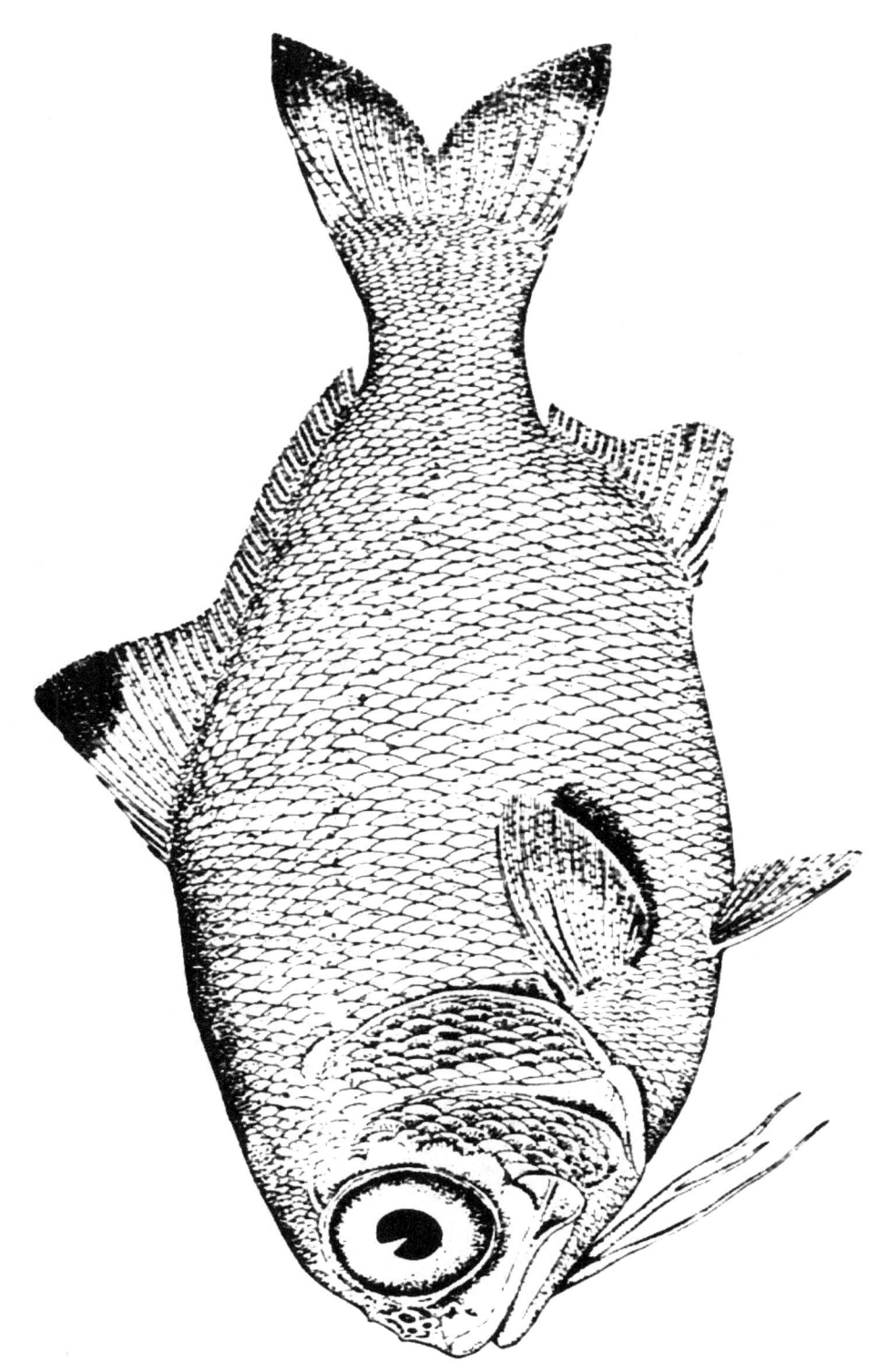

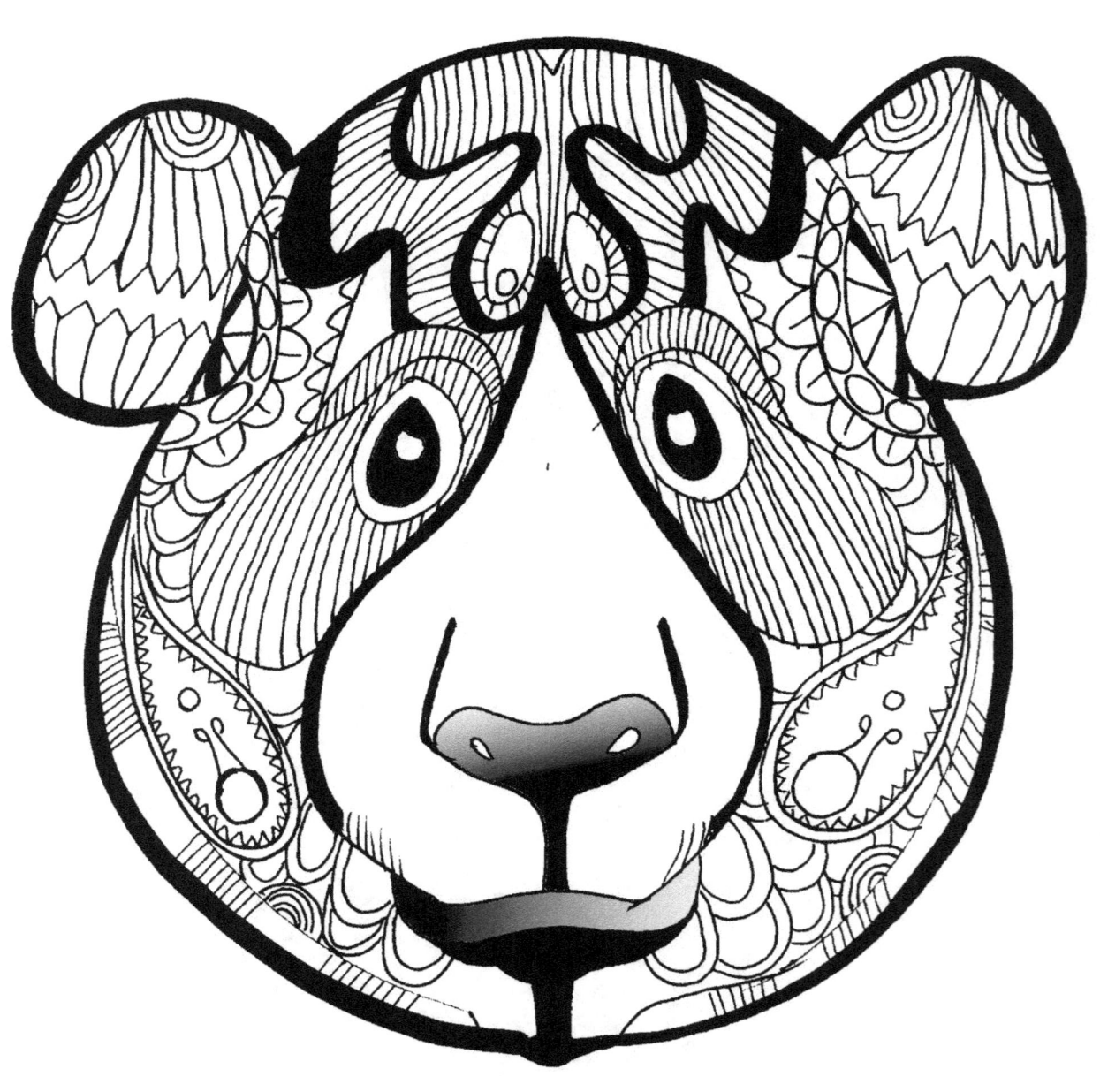

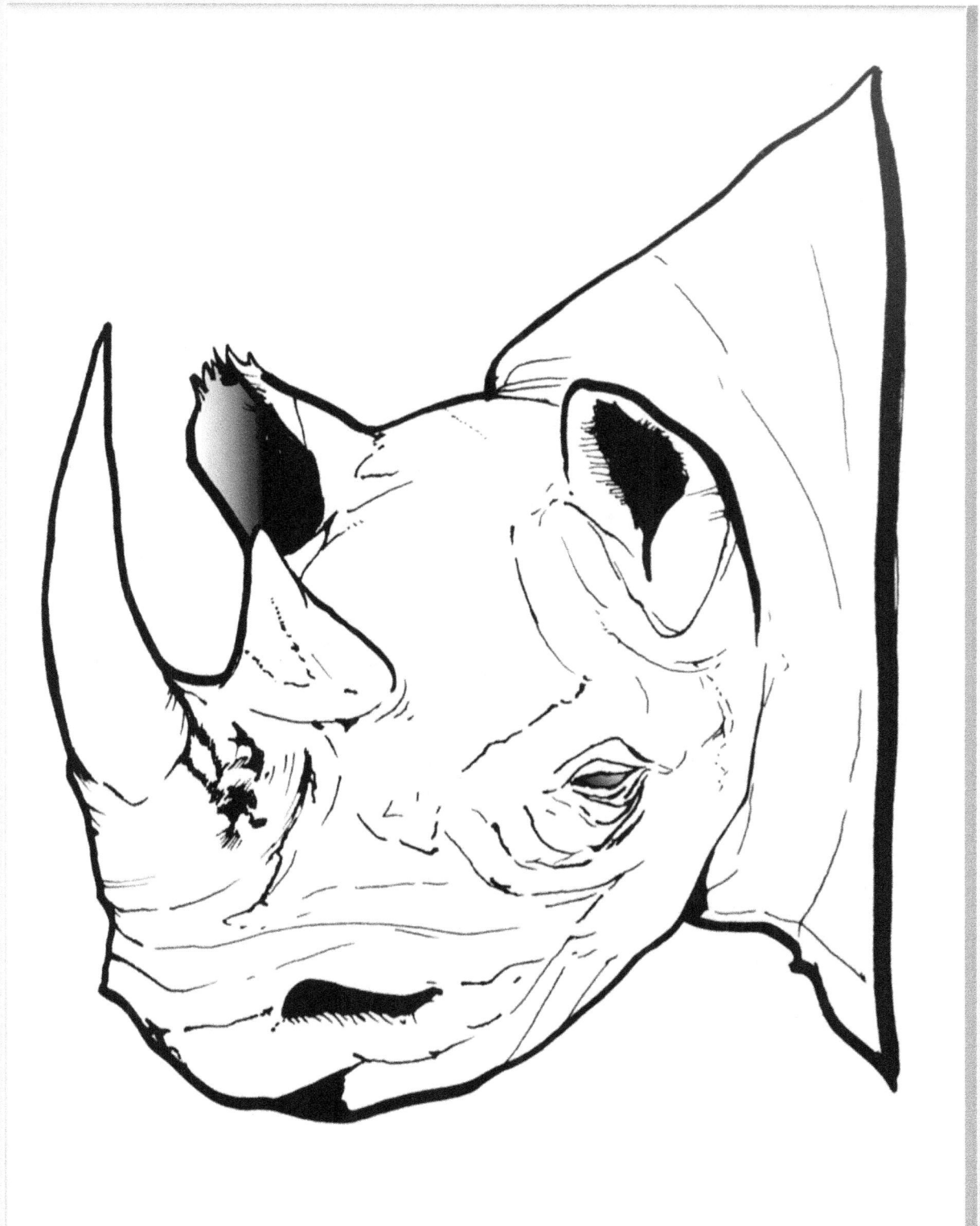

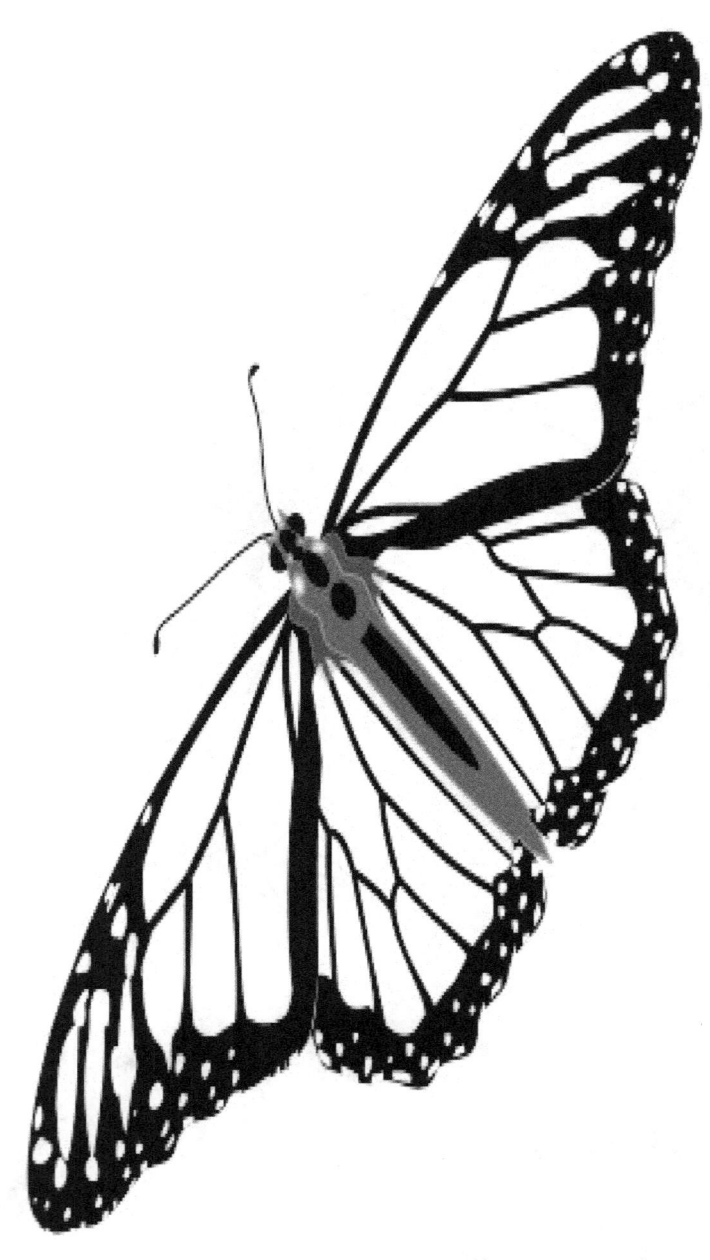

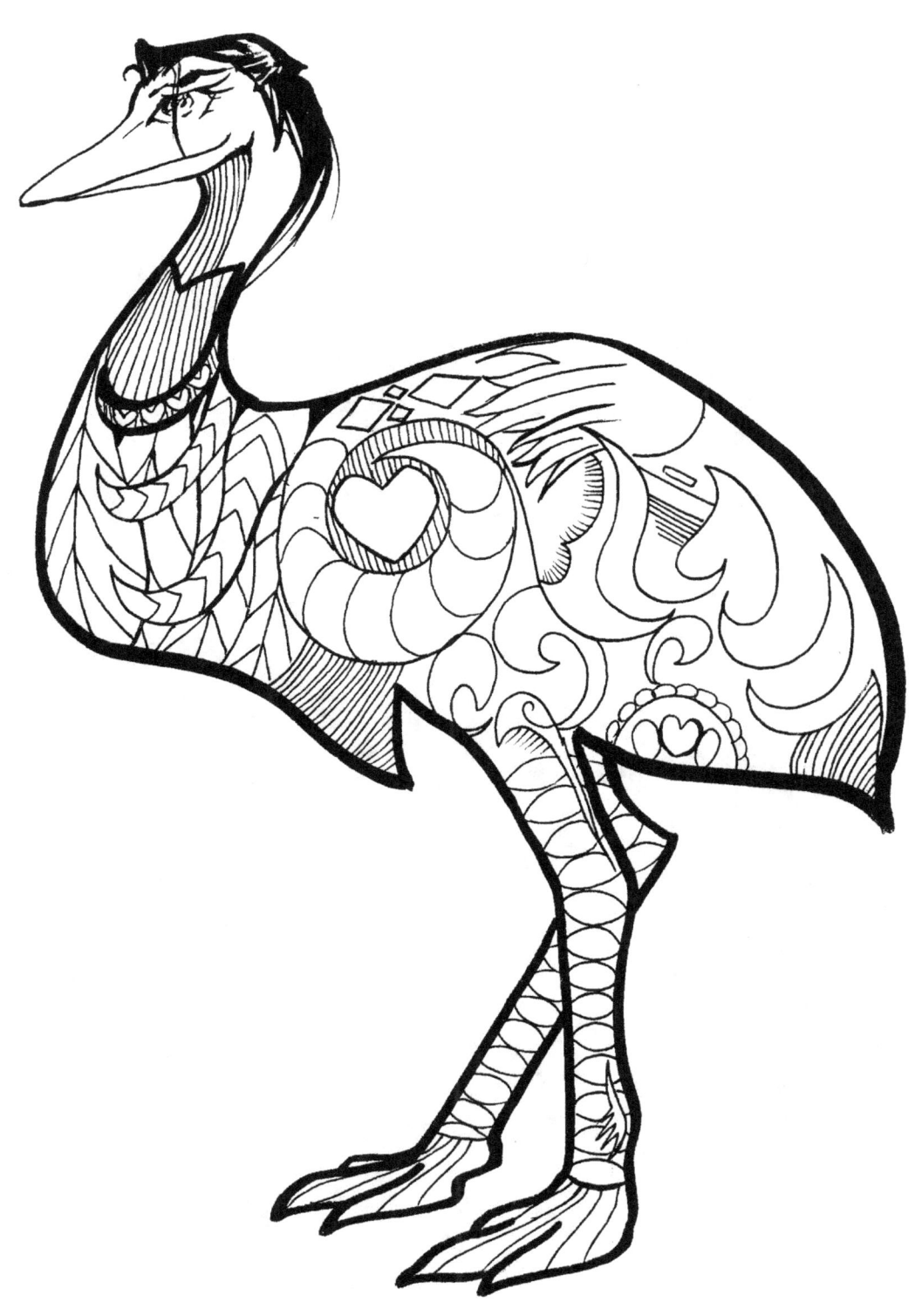

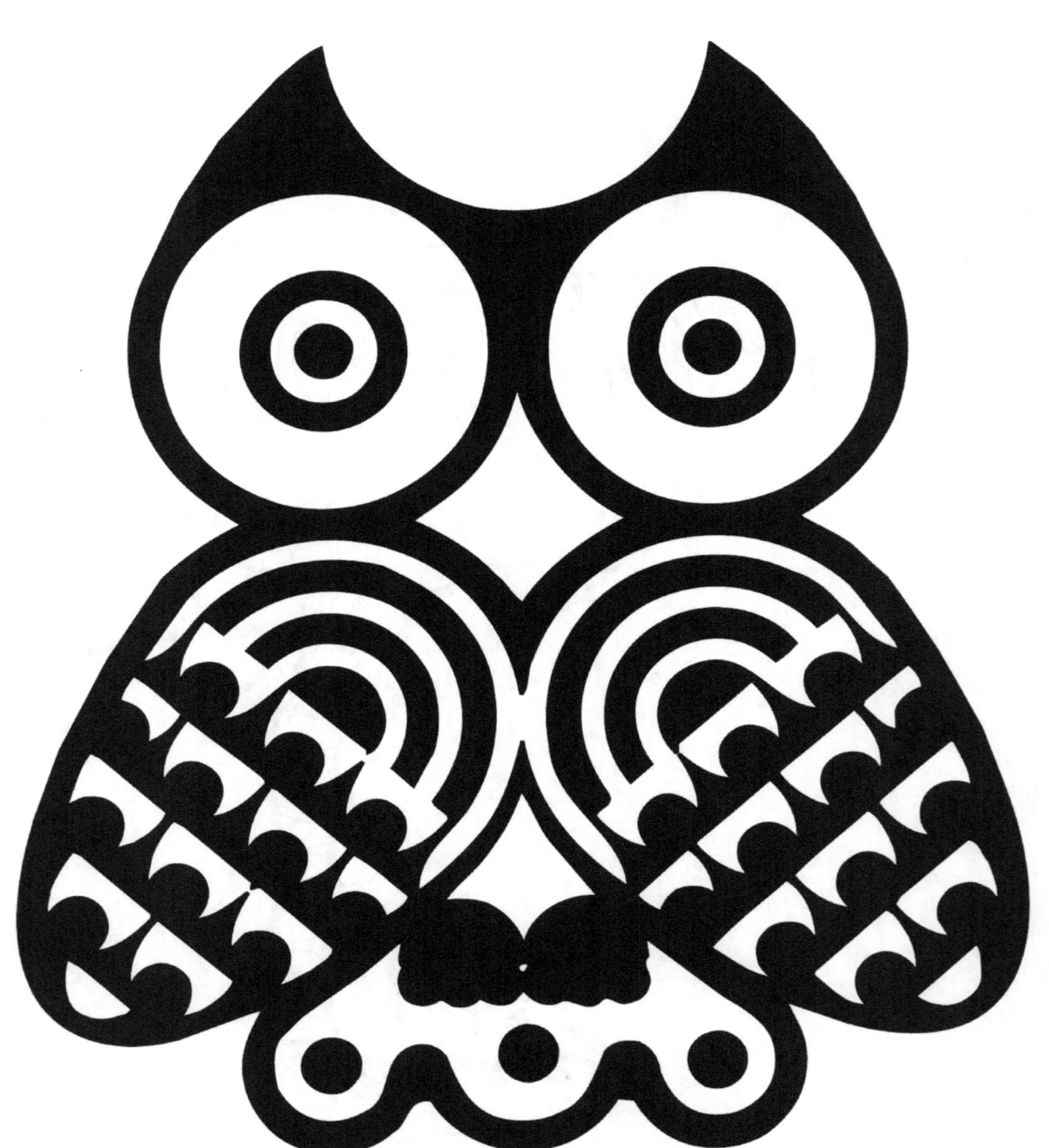

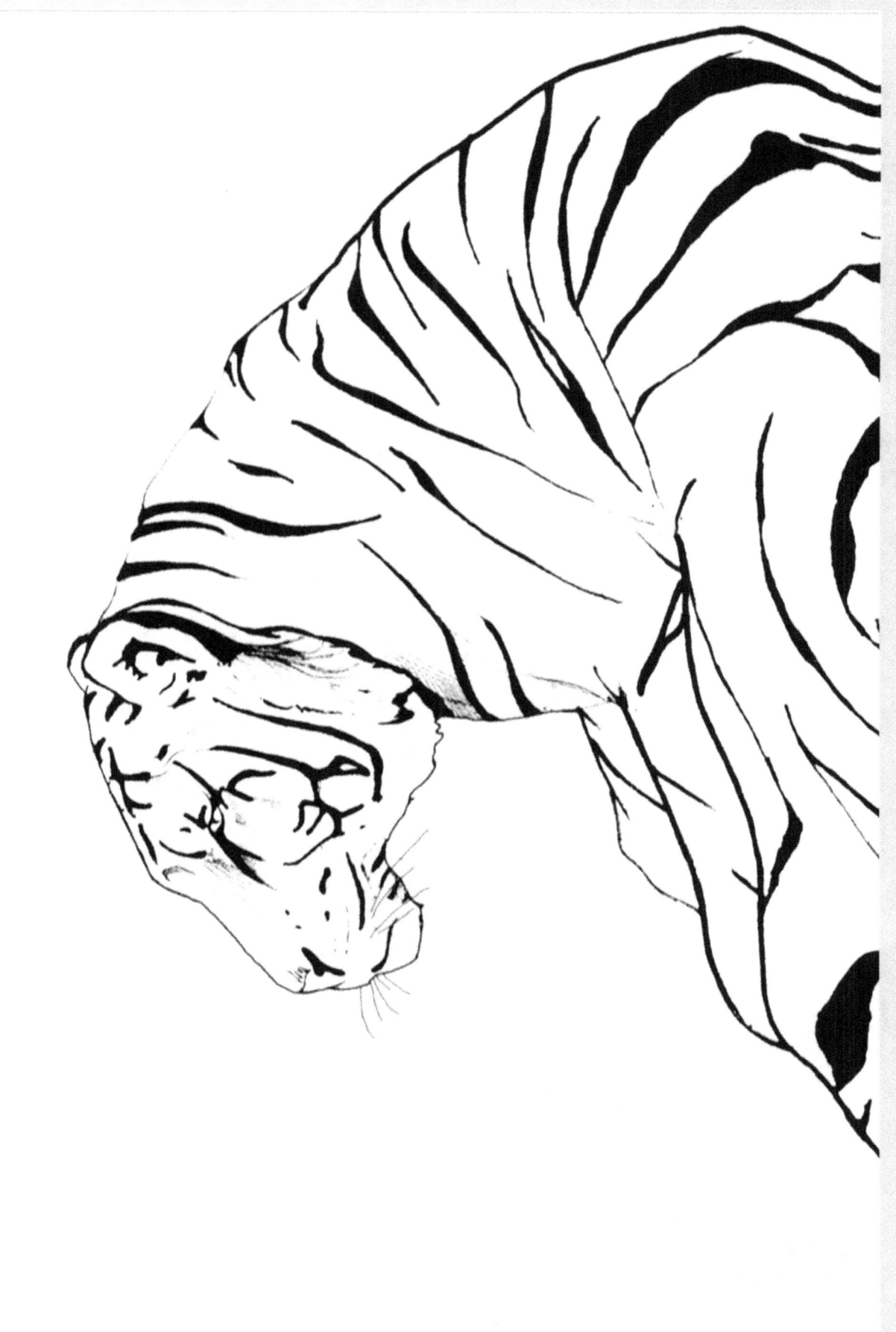

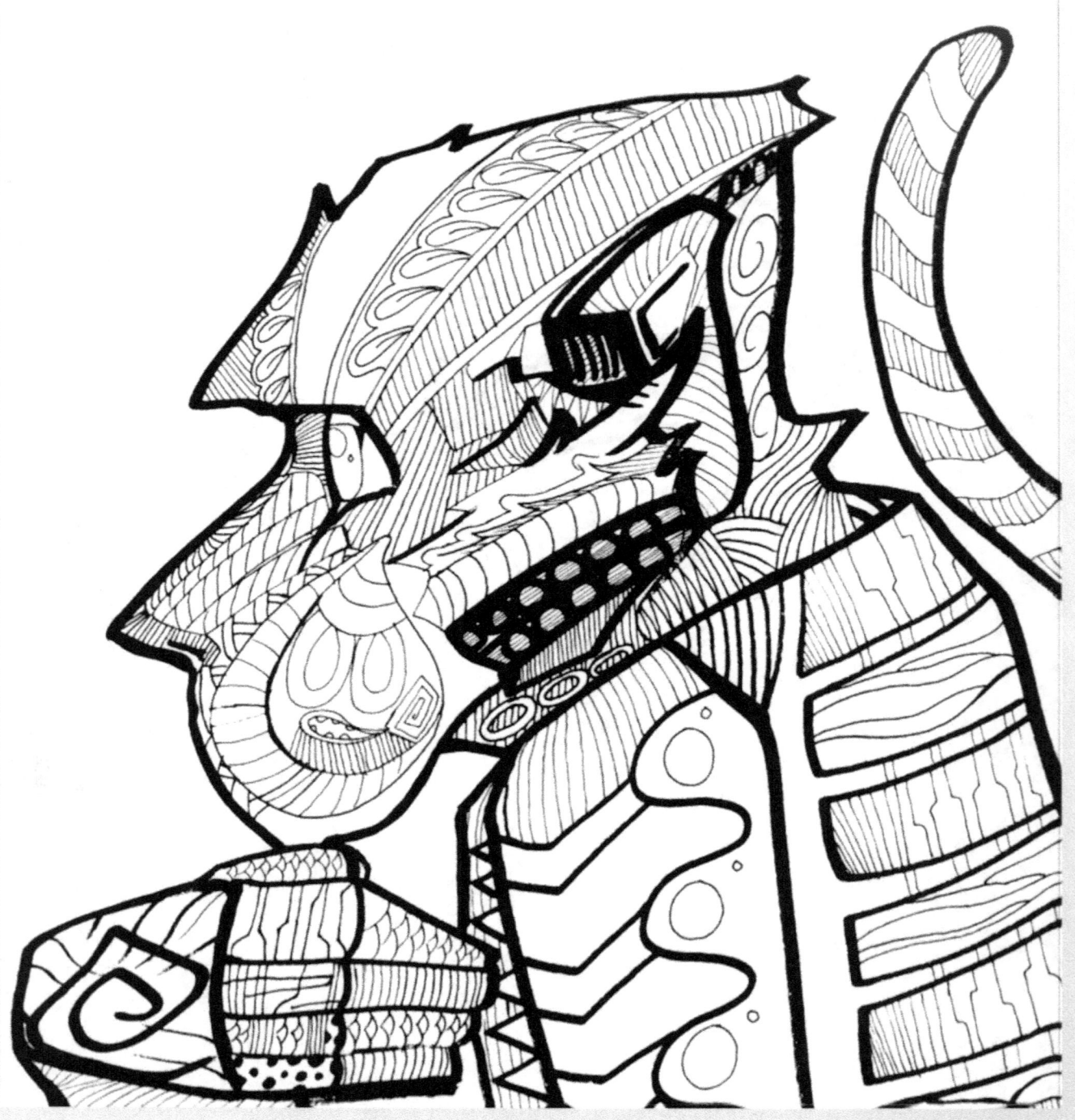

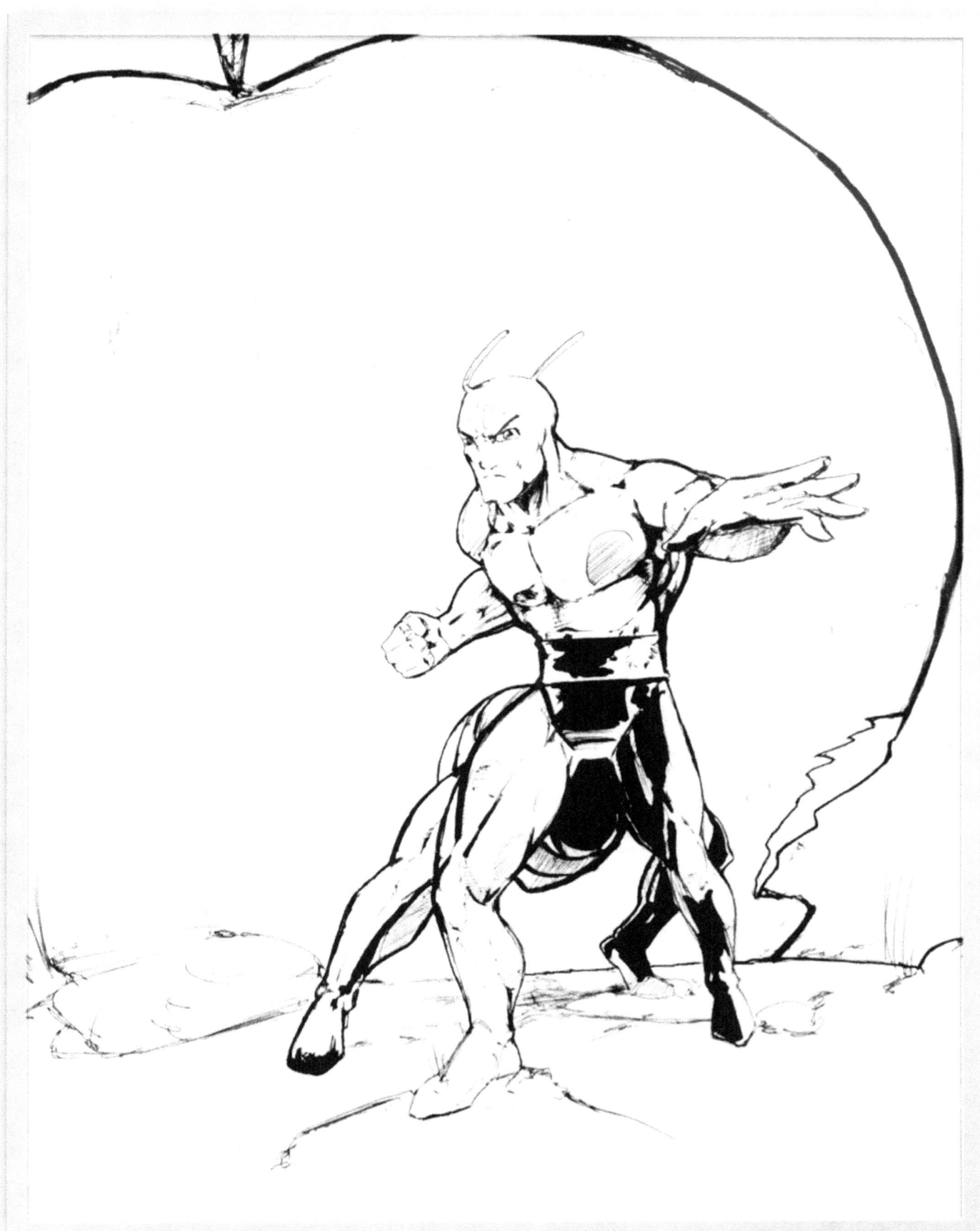

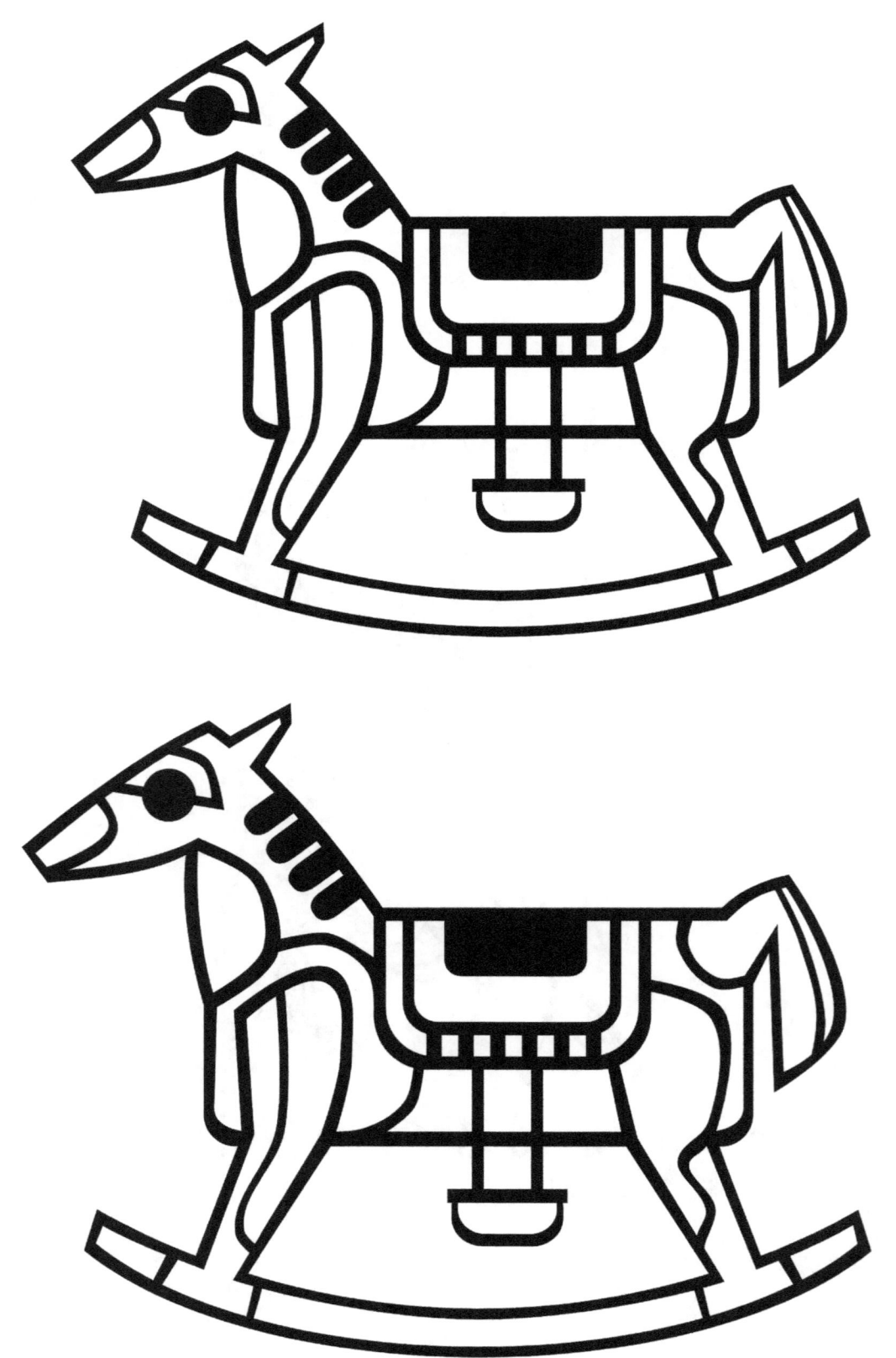

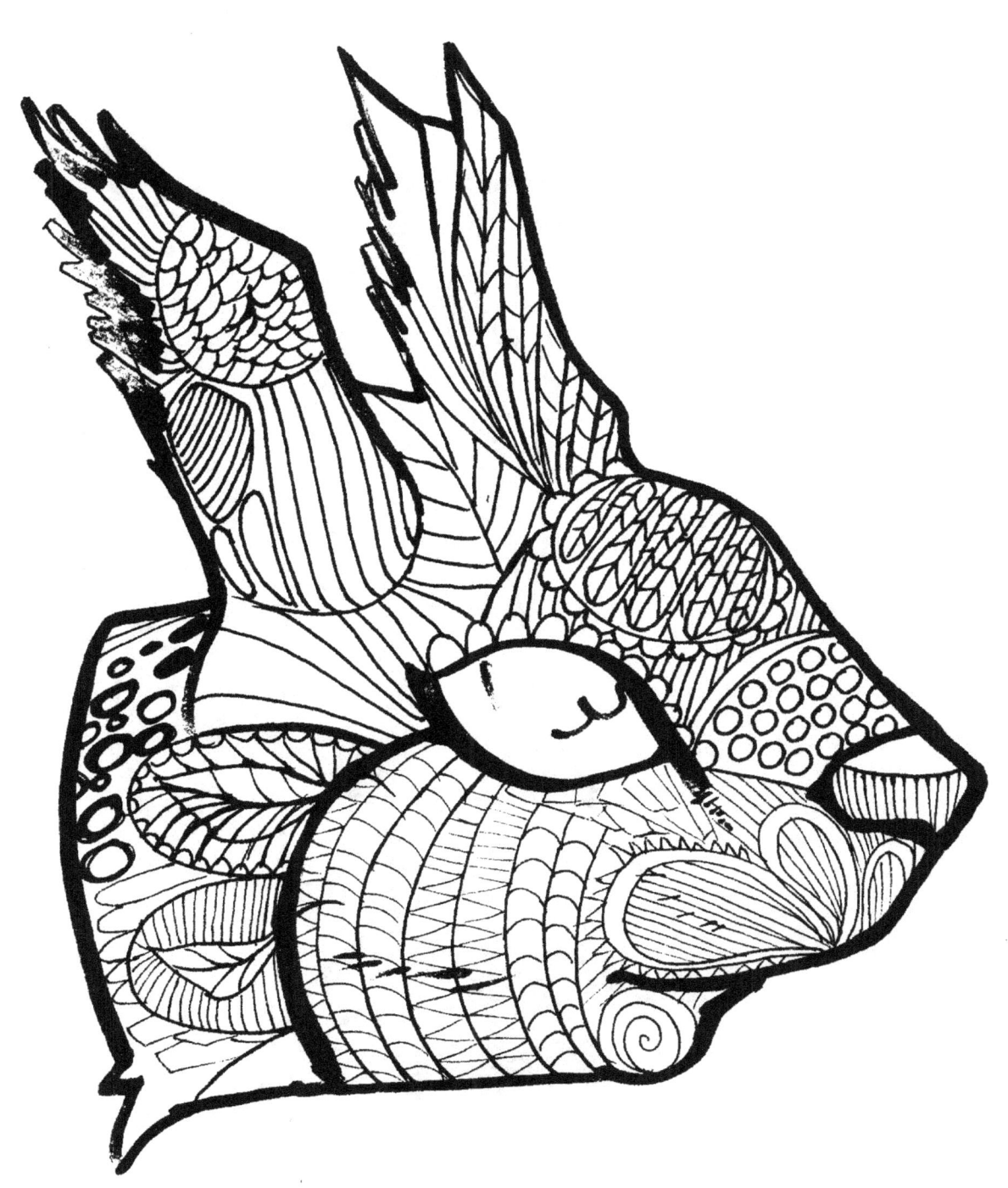

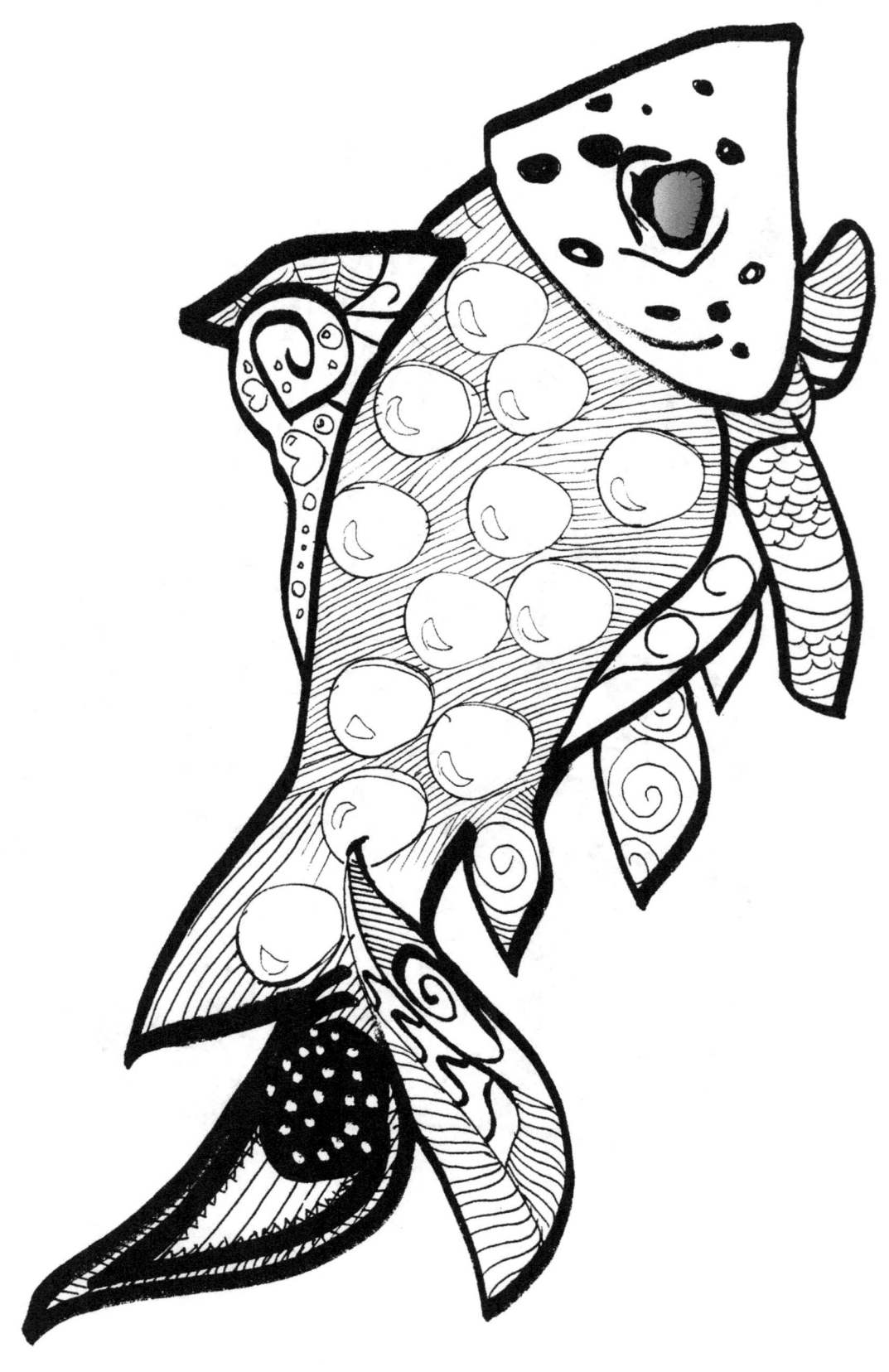

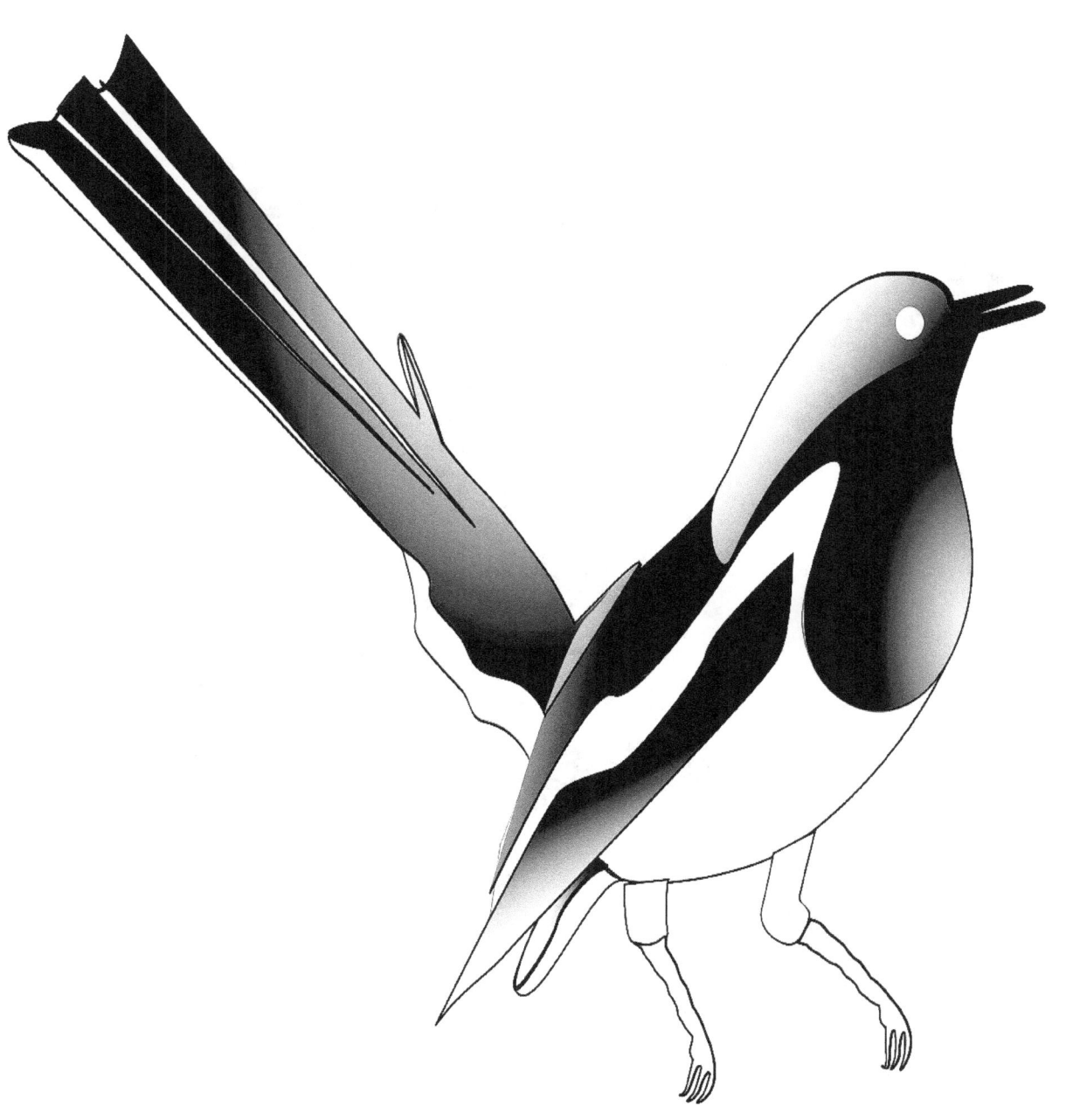

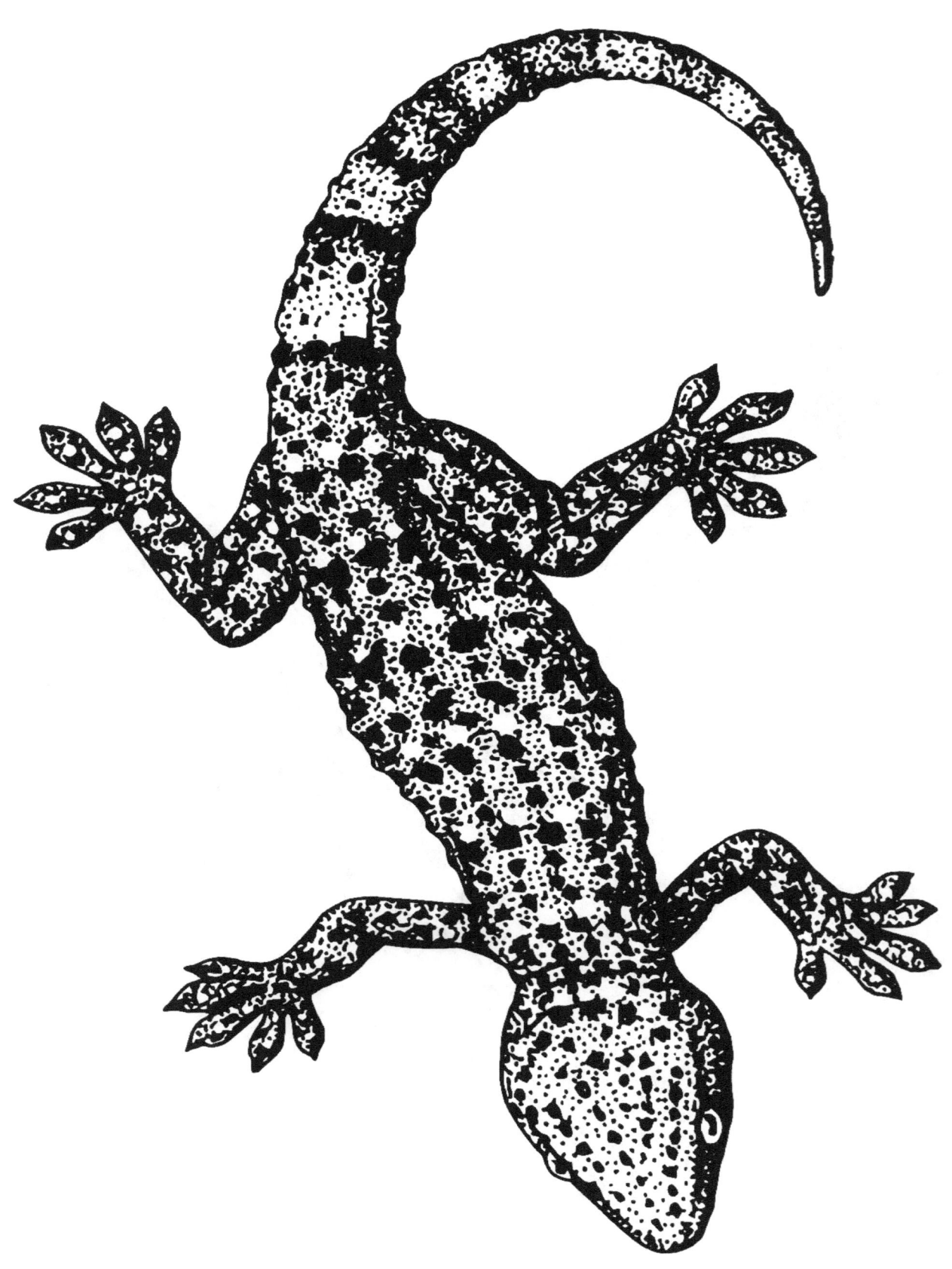

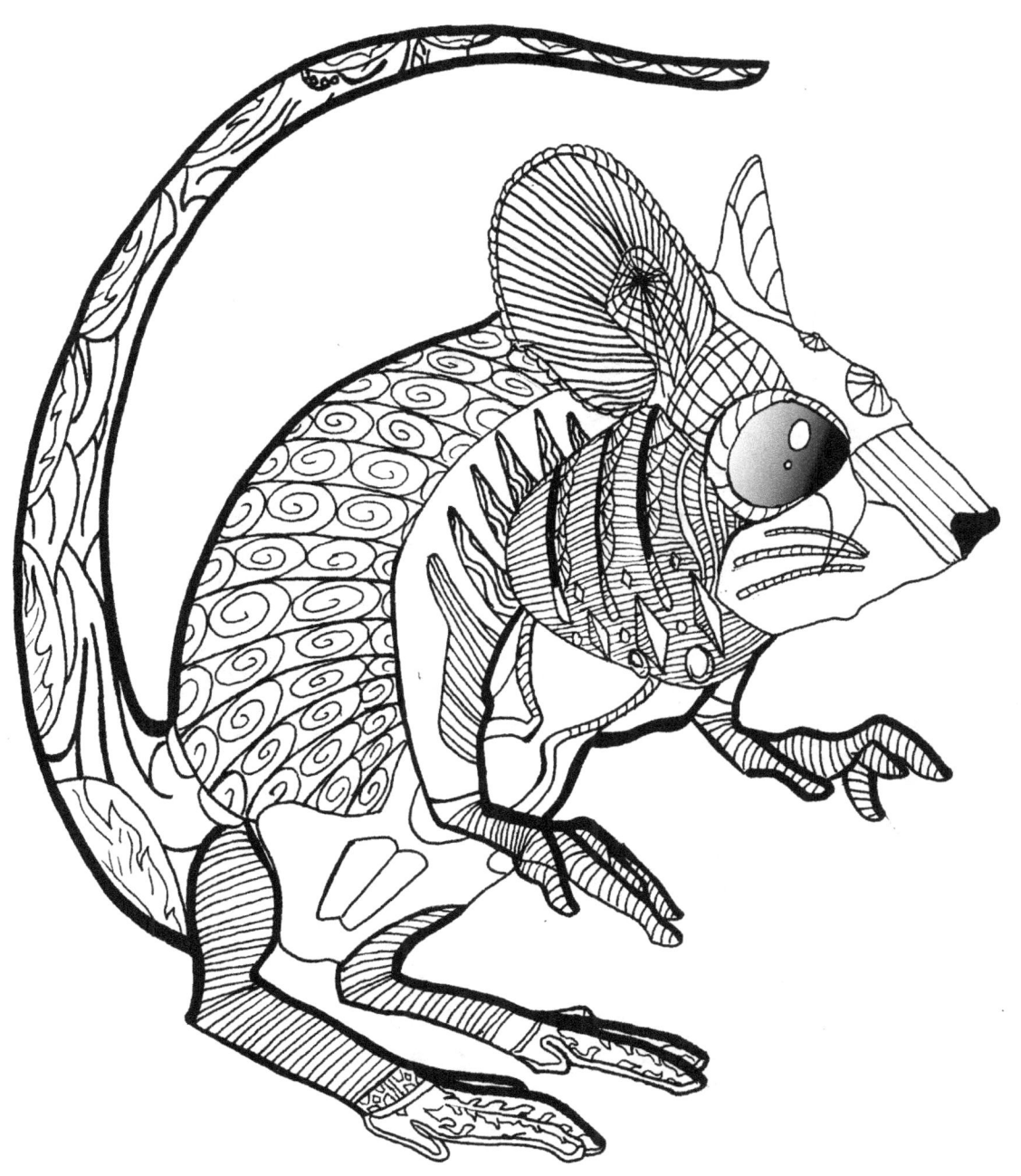

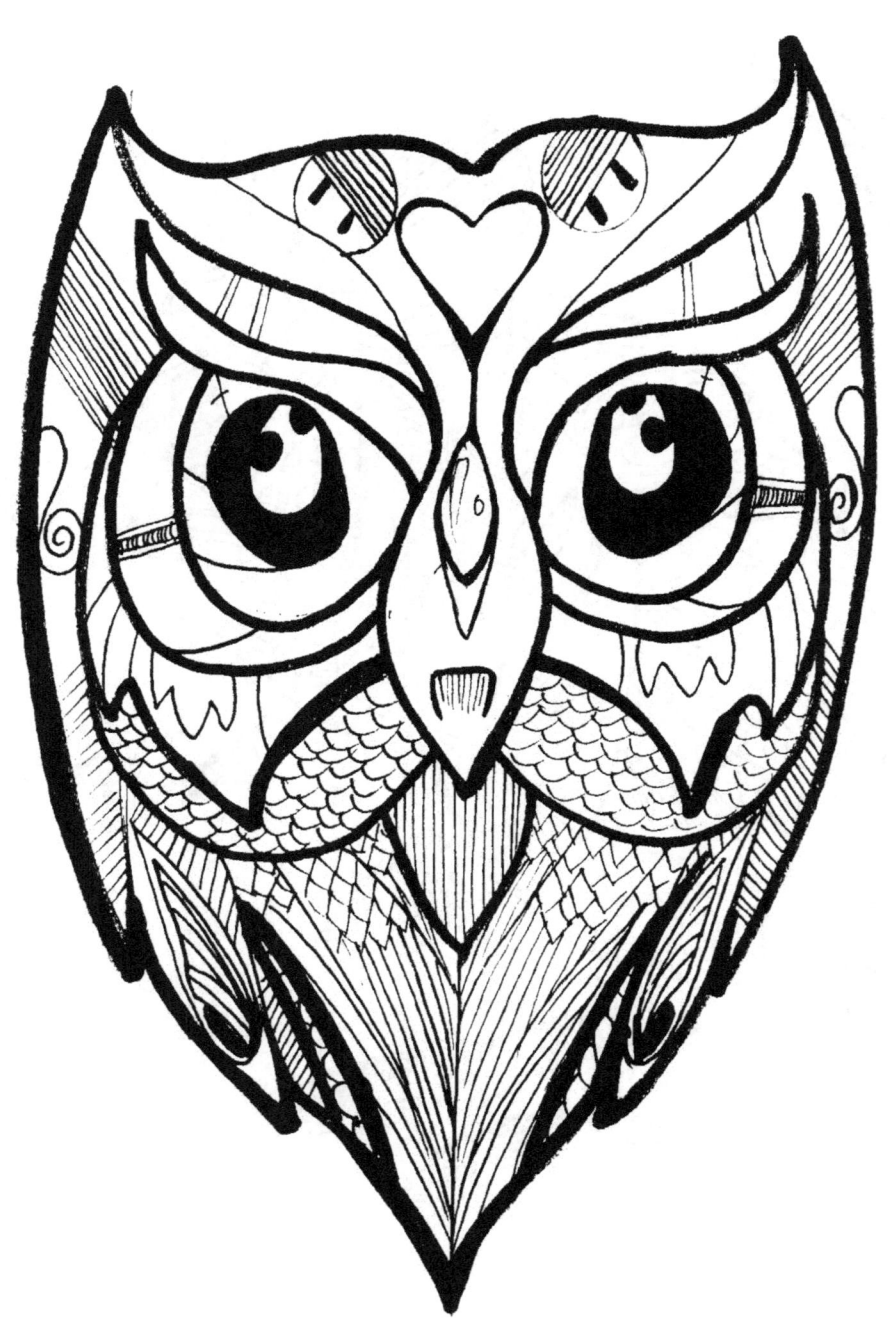

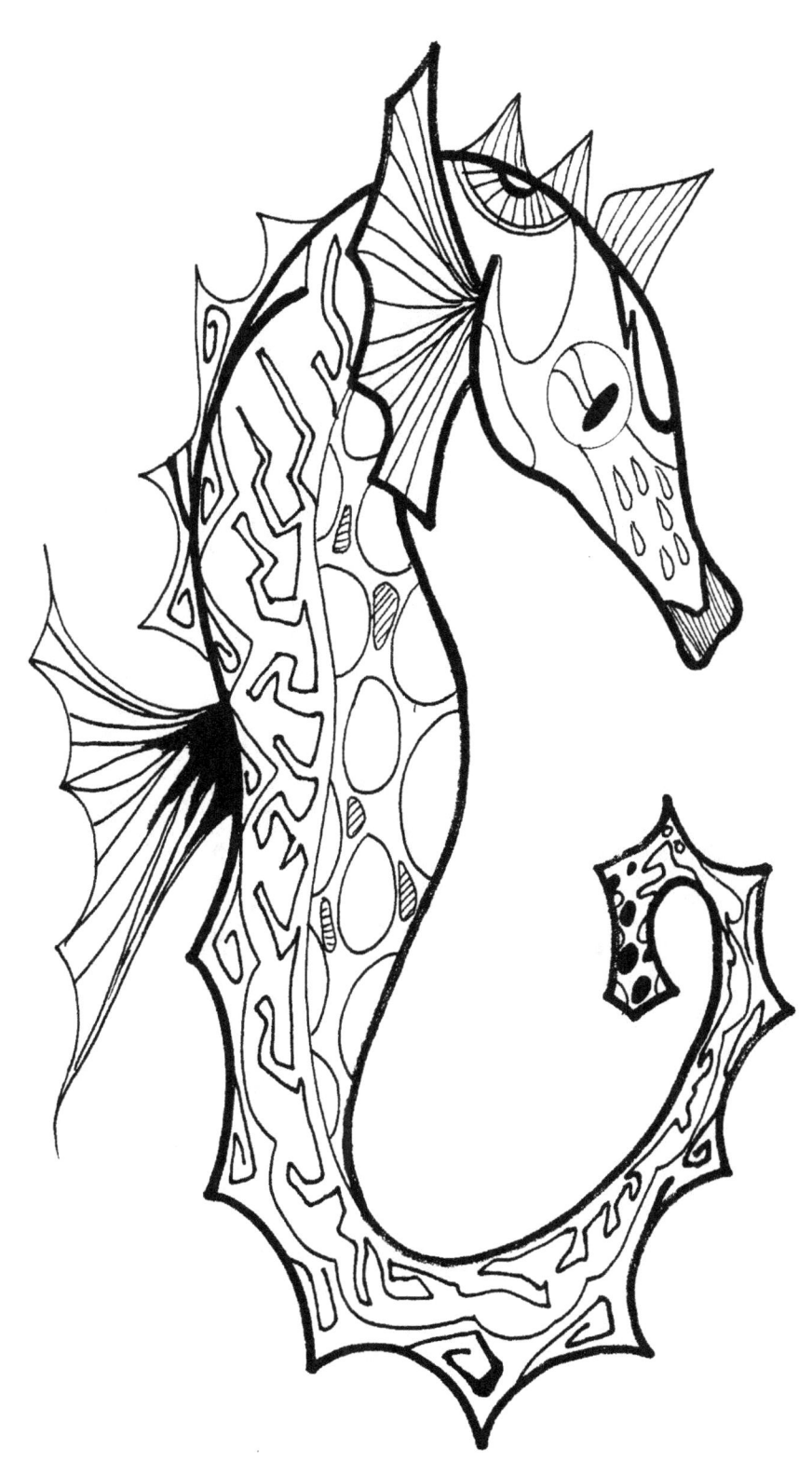

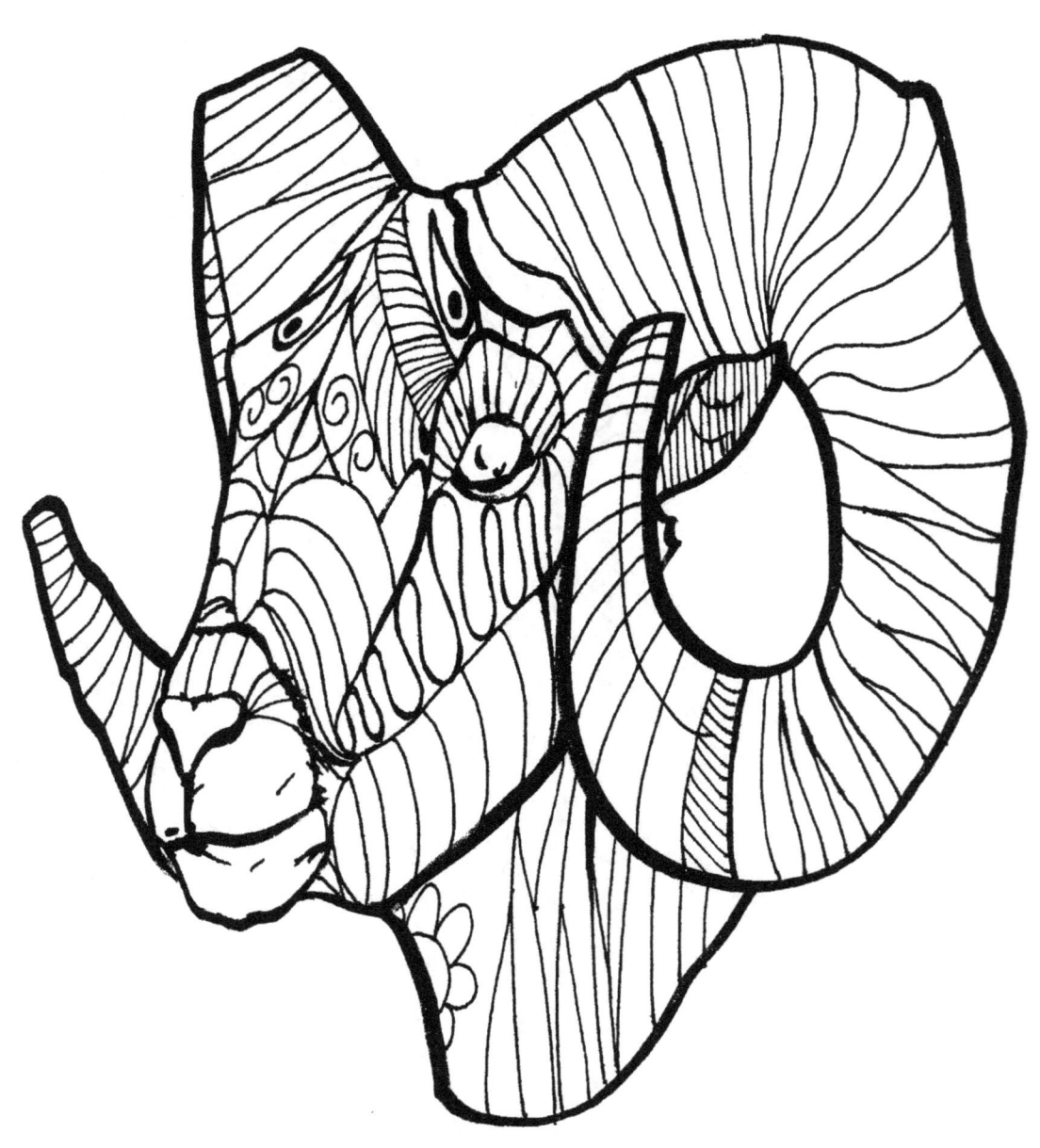

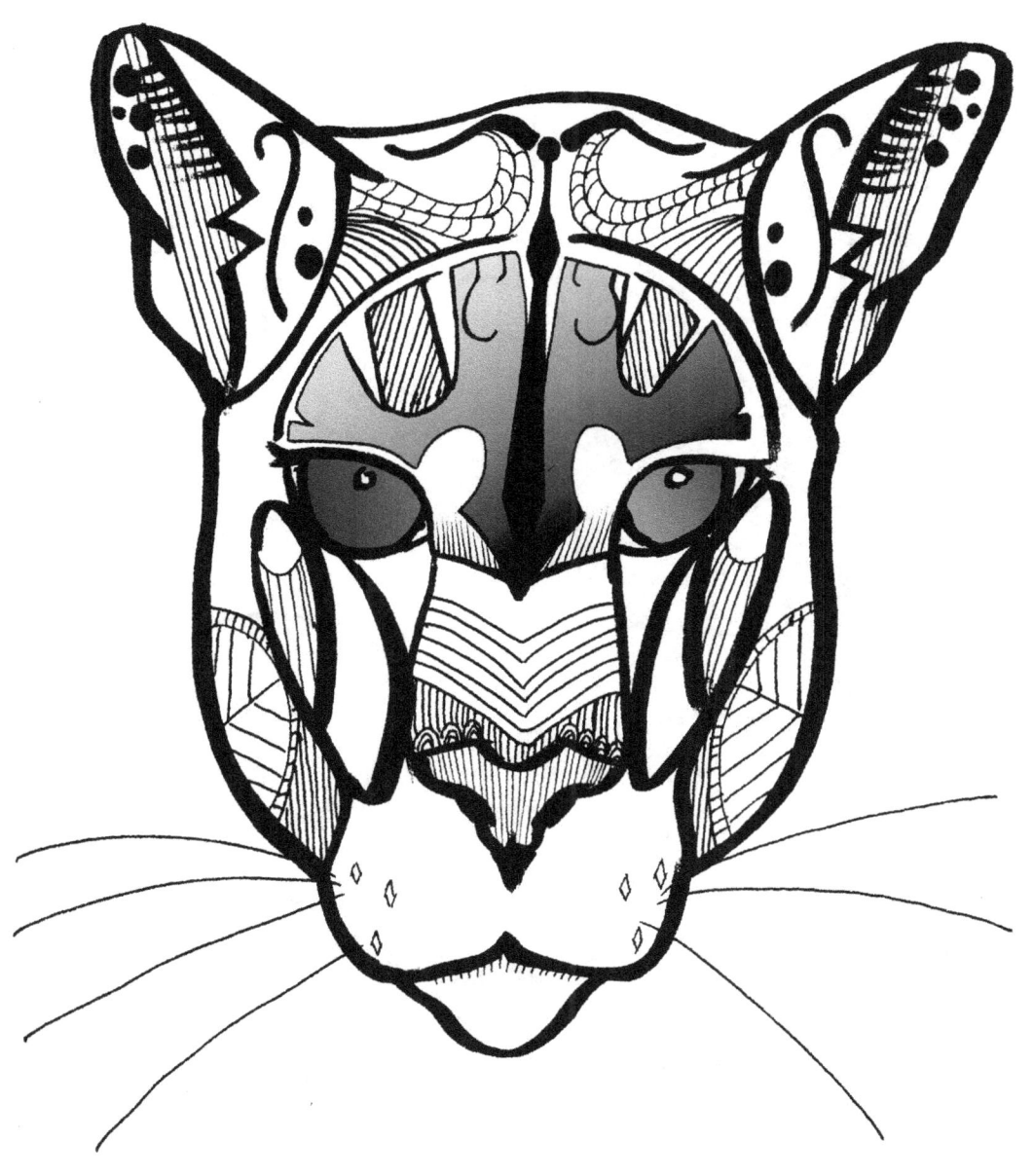

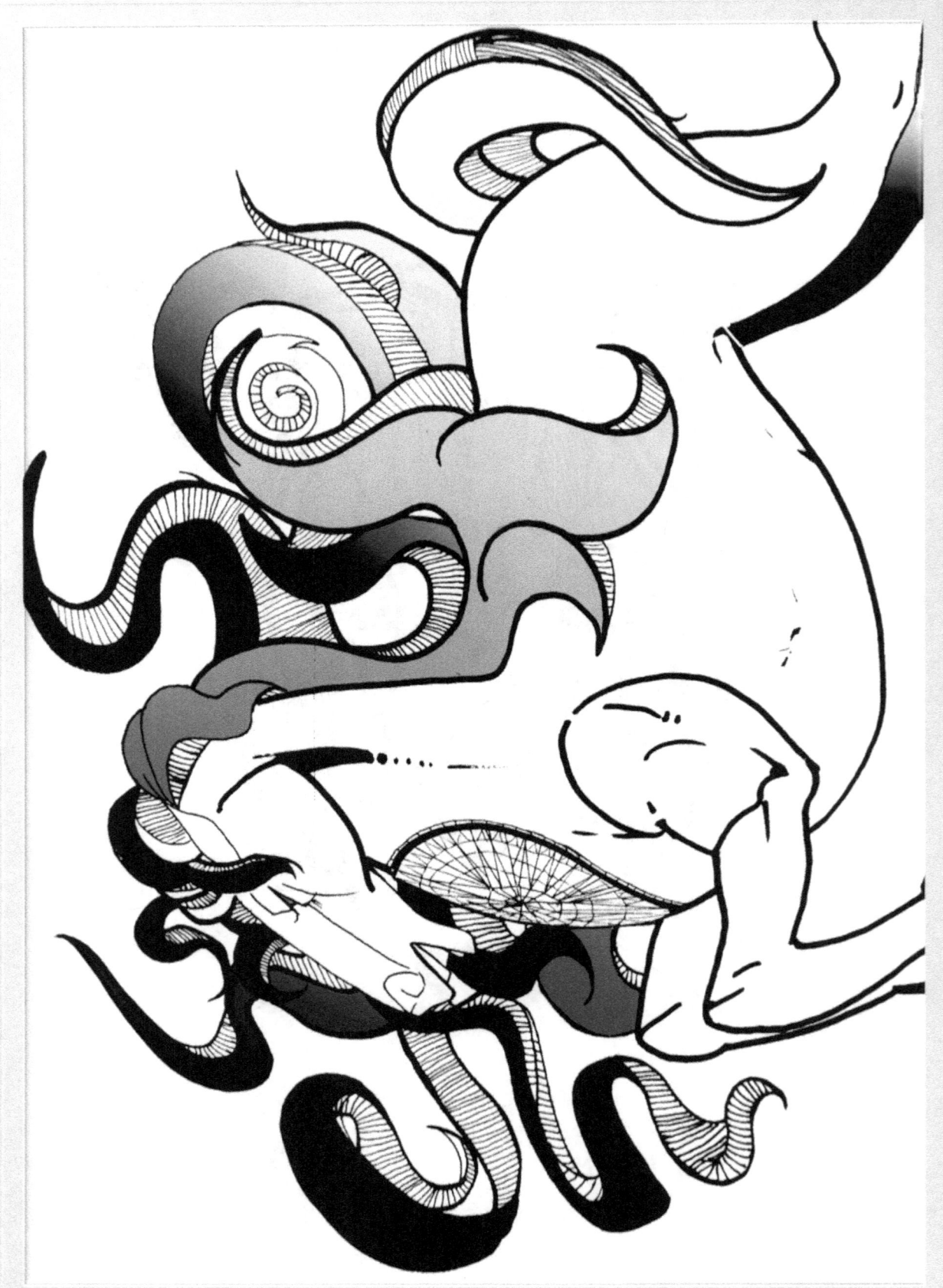

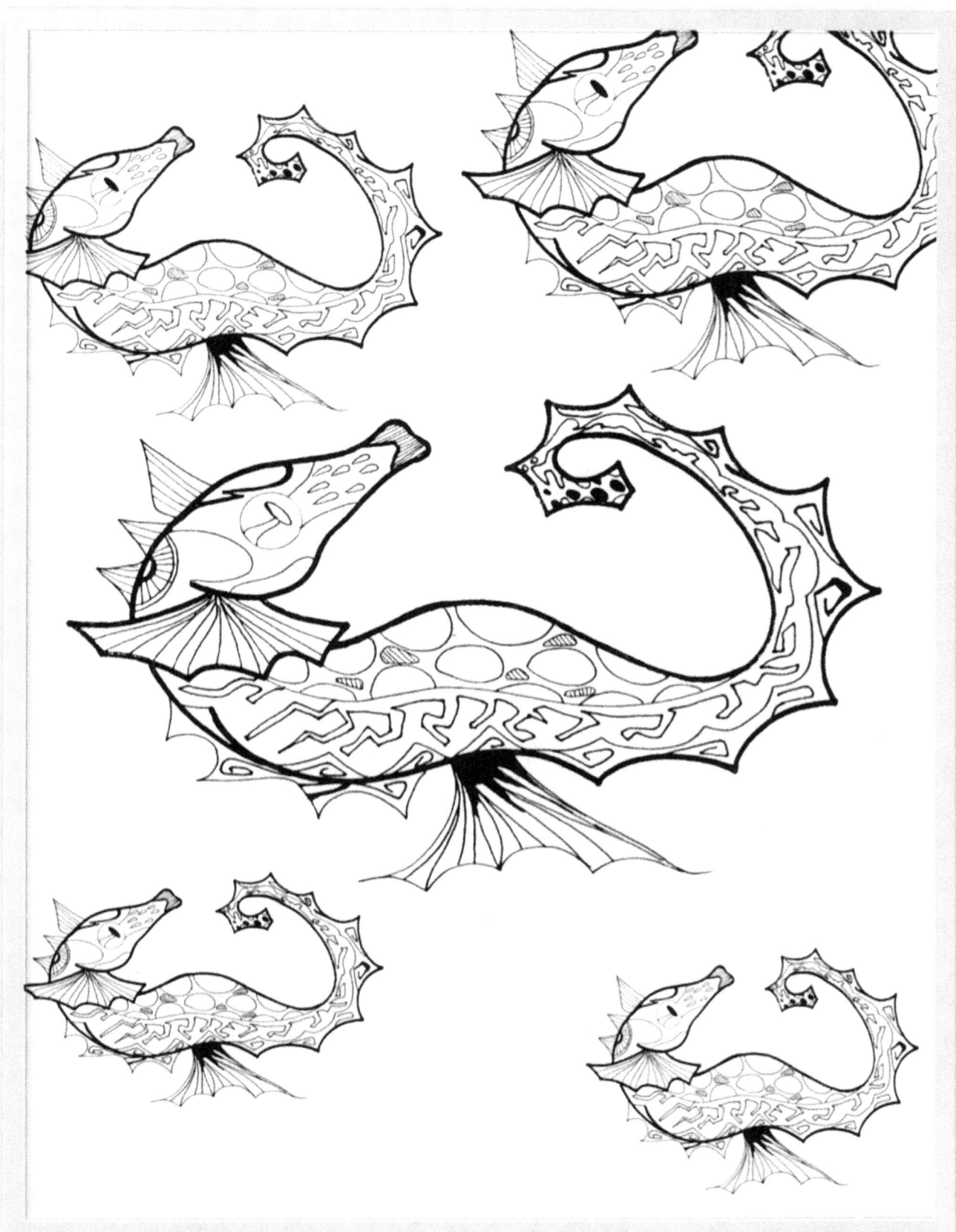

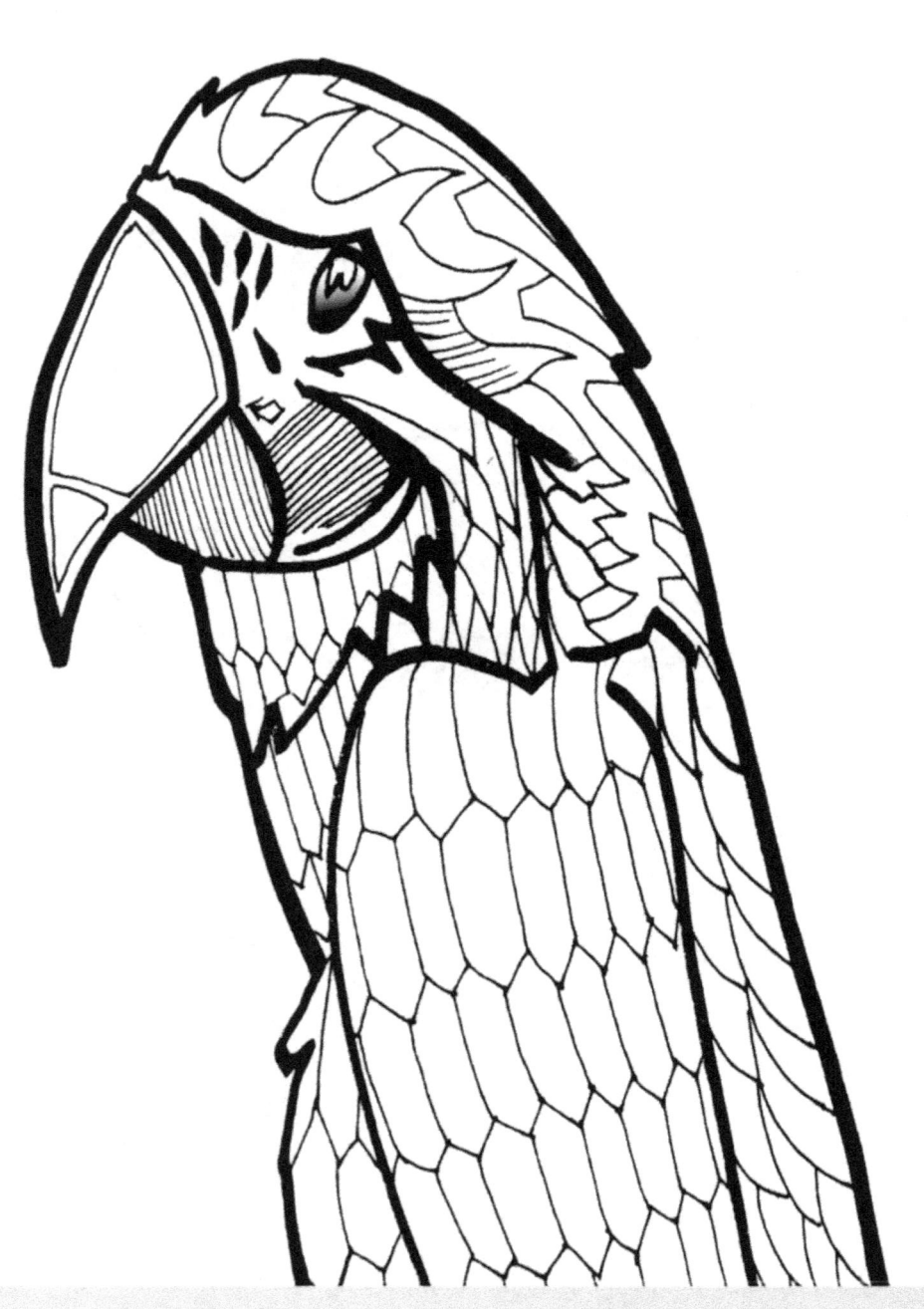

Color Options

Crimson

Red is the color or power. It is related to fire and blood so it's usually related to passion, conviction, strength, love or want. Crimson is a powerful psychological shade, which signifies Risk or Stop and attracts focus. Red has been demonstrated to evoke including raising blood pressure or growing respiration, natural body reactions. Crimson is such a versatile shade as it's used to reveal fire, desire and love while in the exact same time, wrath, risk and stop.

Yellow

Yellow is a color usually related to energy, joy and happiness. Yellow is frequently used to market children's products. Yellow in marketing is utilized to emphasize the main aspects of layout or your product. Yellow should be utilized for lighthearted things but not usually for high end products.

Orange

Orange is a mixture of yellowish and red. The energy of red and well-being of yellowish form a color that symbolizes success, well-being, creativity, excitement and encouragement. It's a citrus color so it's related to stimulate desires and wholesome food. Orange is also the color for endurance and strength. It ought to be utilized to get focus or emphasize significant elements of layout or your product. Orange is an excellent shade for boosting kids 's playthings and food.

Green

The color green is usually related to nature. You consider freshness, fertility, harmony, development, and cash when you see green. Additionally it is a security color, which is connected with «Go» or «great». You need to use green if you are attempting to encourage feelings of trust or security. If you are attempting to encourage environmentally friendly products, green should likewise be utilized.

From the Author

Thank you for buying and coloring our book, we sincerely hope you have enjoyed it!

Can we ask for a small favor? A lot of work goes in to preparing and publishing our books and honest reviews really do help us, especially when it comes to understanding what we should improve in our books.

If you have a minute or less, we would love it if you could leave a review.

We can't wait to here your feed back!

FREE BONUS !

Please do not for get your free gift.
Please download your free Adult Coloring book and free E-book.
You will be able to print the coloring book out and the E-book will be available on any computer or digital smart device. Just go to.

www.syanluz.gr8.com